Reading Achievement
Comprehension Activities to Promote Essential Reading Skills

Grade 7

by
Darriel Ledbetter, M.S.
and
Leland Graham, Ph.D.

Table of Contents

Introduction

Welcome to the **Reading Achievement** series! Each book in this series is designed to reinforce the reading skills appropriate for each grade level and to encourage high-level thinking skills. Because reading is an essential part of all disciplines, mastery of these skills can help students succeed in all academic areas. In addition, experiencing success in reading can increase a student's self-esteem and motivate him or her to read more, both in and out of the classroom.

Each **Reading Achievement** book offers challenging questions for students to answer in response to a variety of grade-level appropriate passages. Various types of reading passages are represented in this book, including fiction, nonfiction, poetry, maps, charts and graphs, and recipes. The format and questions are similar to those found on standardized reading tests. The experience students gain from answering questions in this format may help increase their test scores. In addition, these exercises can be used to enhance your school-adopted reading program, to individualize instruction, to provide extra practice for home schoolers, or to review skills between grades.

> The following reading skills are covered within this book:
>
> - **cause and effect**
> - **comprehension**
> - **critical thinking**
> - **figurative language**
> - **following directions**
> - **main ideas/details**
> - **reference materials**
> - **sequencing**
> - **vocabulary**
> - **true or false**
> - **compare and contrast**

Each **Reading Achievement** book contains additional features to enhance usability. Four pretests, in standardized test format, have been included at the beginning of each book. The pretests have been designed so that they may be used individually, as four stand-alone tests, or in groups. Another convenient feature is a scoring box on each activity page. This scoring box can be programmed to suit your specific classroom and student needs with total problems, total correct, and score.

3

Read the passage. Circle the letter beside each correct answer.

The 2000 Summer Olympics were held in Sydney, Australia. Australia is in the Southern Hemisphere between the Indian and South Pacific oceans. It is not only a country, but also a continent. As a continent, it is the smallest one in the world, but as a country, it is the sixth largest.

More than 18.7 million people live in Australia. The first Australians were Aborigines. Aborigines are descendents of the native people who lived there thousands of years before Europeans arrived. One of their customs is painting their bodies. Different paintings tell different stories. Some identify members of the same tribe or family. Many Aborigines paint themselves for ceremonies and dances. Today, less than 2 percent of the population is Aboriginal. Now, most Australians are of European descent. Captain James Cook claimed Australia for Great Britain in 1770. Many of the first colonists were prisoners who were sentenced to live there far from their homes in England. For a long time, mainly British and Irish people moved to Australia, but after World War II people from many different countries began moving there.

Many unique Australian animals belong to a group called "marsupials." This group includes kangaroos, wallabies, koalas, and bandicoots. Almost all the mammals native to Australia are marsupials. They carry and feed their young in pouches and are nocturnal.

You are probably familiar with the Tasmanian devil from cartoons. But did you know that there is really an animal by that name? It is a small, black and white marsupial that lives on the island of Tasmania, which is just off the coast of Australia. Tasmanian devils are rather shy, but they growl and scream so loudly at night that settlers thought the woods were filled with horrible creatures.

1. This story is about:
   A. the 2000 Summer Olympics
   B. the people and animals of Australia
   C. Aborigines
   D. the Tasmanian Devil

2. From reading this story, you might compare Aborigines to:
   A. Tasmanians
   B. Europeans
   C. Native Americans
   D. Irish

3. The animal known as the Tasmanian devil might have gotten its name from:
   A. the way it looks
   B. the horrible night noises it makes
   C. a cartoon
   D. Captain James Cook

4. The word "descendent" in this story means:
   A. relative
   B. dead person
   C. bandicoot
   D. explorer

5. Many of the first colonists came to Australia because:
   A. They came as tourists and decided to stay.
   B. They were prisoners.
   C. They were born there.
   D. They liked the scenery.

| Total Problems: | Total Correct: | Score: |

Read each passage. Circle the letter beside the correct answer.

Manicuring and coloring fingernails are certainly not recent beauty practices. Archaeologists excavating at the royal tombs at Ur of the Chaldees in Babylonia discovered a gold manicure set used by someone in the year 3200 B.C. That would make it over five thousand years old.

Ancient queens like Nefertiti and Cleopatra of Egypt, painted their fingernails and toenails different shades of red to make them more beautiful. For hundreds of years, the upper-class women of Spain also used color on their nails. It seems that history's most cultured women have recognized nail care as being important to their beauty and attractiveness. One wonders what Cleopatra and Nefertiti would think about multicolored nails and nail decals and jewels.

1. The best title for this story is:
    A. Beauty Practices in History   B. Colorful Nails Are Not New
    C. Cleopatra and Nefertiti   D. Archaeological Discoveries

2. Having one's nails done appears to be a practice that is how old?
    A. 3200 years   B. over 5000 years   C. 50 years   D. just a few years

3. How do we know that ancient queens had their nails manicured?
    A Archaeologists found their nail polish bottles.
    B. Archaeologists found artificial nails in the tombs.
    C. Archaeologists found a gold manicure set in a tomb.
    D. Archaeologists found mummies with manicured nails.

4. Which sentence states an opinion?
    A. Manicuring and coloring fingernails are certainly not recent beauty practices.
    B. That would make it over five thousand years old.
    C. For hundreds of years, the upper-class women of Spain also used color on their nails.
    D. It seems that history's most cultured women have recognized nail care as being important to their beauty and attractiveness.

Saltwater taffy is a popular confection that was developed completely by accident. David Bradley owned a store on the boardwalk in Atlantic City, New Jersey in 1883. His taffy was badly damaged when it got soaked during a storm. A little girl came in the next morning asking for taffy, to which Mr. Bradley disgustedly replied that this was "saltwater taffy." Instead of being disappointed, the little girl thought the "new" candy was delicious, and soon other children wanted some of that wonderful new candy. A bit of advertising and word-of-mouth spread the news. Today, it is estimated that thousands of pounds of saltwater taffy are sold every summer day in Atlantic City, and this delicious accident tantalizes taste buds all over the world.

5. This story is about:
    A. a storm in Atlantic City   B. an accident on the boardwalk
    C. how saltwater taffy was invented   D. why it is important to advertise candy

Read the passage. Circle the letter beside each correct answer.

Obtain a set of four rubber balls of equal size and weight. Begin by throwing just one ball straight up in the air with your right hand and catching it with the same hand. Repeat this several times, throwing the ball about a foot high and as straight as possible. Follow the same procedure with your left hand. When you've conquered that exercise, toss the ball with your right hand, giving it a slight left arch; catch it with your left hand and toss it back to your right. Next take two balls, holding one in each hand. Toss the ball from your right hand, flip the ball from your left hand to your right, catch the ball with your left, and continue the cycle. Work your way up to three, and then four balls.

1. These directions tell you how to:
   A. throw a ball straight   B. catch a baseball
   C. serve a tennis ball   D. juggle

2. The first thing you should do, after finding four balls, is:
   A. Toss a ball with your right hand and catch it with your left.
   B. Work your way up to three, and then four balls.
   C. Throw one ball straight up and catch it with the same hand.
   D. Flip the ball.

3. When using two balls, after you toss the ball from your right hand, you should:
   A. Drop the other one.
   B. Flip the ball from your left hand to your right.
   C. Try to hit it with the other ball.
   D. Bounce the ball.

In the following excerpts from restaurant reviews, you will find examples of figurative language. Select the best meaning for the boldfaced expression.

4. Lately, though, the cooking seems to have lost some of its polish; it's **intriguing but uneven**. The cooking is:
   A. interesting but not dependably good
   B. good, but not cooked completely
   C. good, but not served well
   D. interesting, but it doesn't look good

5. This hangout takes wrap-making to a new level of creativity, using tortillas **as colorful as the fillings**. The tortillas are:
   A. not real; this means the paper they are wrapped in
   B. ordinary tortillas
   C. available in different flavors
   D. multicolored

Total Problems: _____   Total Correct: _____   Score: _____

Read the passage. Circle the letter beside each correct answer.

Death Valley Scotty was a rich old man who lived in a castle in Death Valley. Everyone knew he was rich because he would tip waitresses with hundred-dollar bills and throw silver dollars in the street just to watch people scramble for them. No one knew how Scotty got so rich, though. Legend has it that one day Scotty was out in the Panamint Mountains with his favorite mule, Betsy. Betsy was feeling mighty jumpy, and wouldn't do what Scotty wanted her to. Finally, he just let the old mule go where she wanted to. She headed up a narrow gorge. It was late after-noon and hot enough to fry an egg on the sand. Suddenly, she stopped and brayed like she was sick. Scotty scratched his head, and said, "Betsy, I think you've gone just about far enough with this foolishness. We're getting out of here." But Betsy wouldn't budge. She got behind Scotty and pushed him into a dry, rocky ravine. He got up, dusted himself off, said a few choice words to Betsy, and looked around. He couldn't believe his eyes. All around him were quartz rocks, and in the quartz were huge chunks of gold. He climbed out of the ravine and kissed Betsy on the nose. From that day on, she was called Gold-Nosed Betsy.

1. This main idea of this story is:
    A. how Death Valley Scotty became rich   B. why Scotty lived in a castle
    C. living in Death Valley   D. how stubborn mules are

2. Betsy was:
    A. Scotty's wife   B. Scotty's daughter
    C. Scotty's favorite mule   D. Scotty's girlfriend

3. When Scotty said, "Betsy, I think you've gone just about far enough with this foolishness," he was probably feeling:
    A. hungry   B. sleepy
    C. hot, tired, and disgusted   D. worried that Betsy was sick

4. In this story, the word ravine means:
    A. a deep gully   B. a wide river   C. a dark cave   D. an old shack

5. If this story is a legend:
    A. it is factual and true
    B. it is gossip
    C. it was found on a map
    D. it has been passed down from person to person

6. When Scotty said a few choice words to Betsy, he was probably:
    A. telling her how smart she was
    B. telling her to go get help
    C. fussing at her for pushing him in the ravine
    D. crying because he was hurt

Total Problems:	Total Correct:	Score:

Page 4

Name _____   Pretest

Read the passage. Circle the letter beside each correct answer.

The 2000 Summer Olympics were held in Sydney, Australia. Australia is in the Southern Hemisphere between the Indian and South Pacific oceans. It is not only a country, but also a continent. As a continent, it is the smallest one in the world, but as a country, it is the sixth largest.

More than 18.7 million people live in Australia. The first Australians were Aborigines. Aborigines are descendents of the native people who lived there thousands of years before Europeans arrived. One of their customs is painting their bodies. Different paintings tell different stories. Some identify members of the same tribe or family. Many Aborigines paint themselves for ceremonies and dances. Today, less than 2 percent of the population is Aboriginal. Now, most Australians are of European descent. Captain James Cook claimed Australia for Great Britain in 1770. Many of the first colonists were prisoners who were sentenced to live there far from their homes in England. For a long time, mainly British and Irish people moved to Australia, but after World War II people from many different countries began moving there.

Many unique Australian animals belong to a group called "marsupials." This group includes kangaroos, wallabies, koalas, and bandicoots. Almost all the mammals native to Australia are marsupials. They carry and feed their young in pouches and are nocturnal.

You are probably familiar with the Tasmanian devil from cartoons. But did you know that there is really an animal by that name? It is a small, black and white marsupial that lives on the island of Tasmania, which is just off the coast of Australia. Tasmanian devils are rather shy, but they growl and scream so loudly at night that settlers thought the woods were filled with horrible creatures.

1. This story is about:
   A. the 2000 Summer Olympics   **B. the people and animals of Australia**
   C. Aborigines   D. the Tasmanian Devil

2. From reading this story, you might compare Aborigines to:
   A. Tasmanians   B. Europeans
   C. Native Americans   D. Irish

3. The animal known as the Tasmanian devil might have gotten its name from:
   A. the way it looks   **B. the horrible night noises it makes**
   C. a cartoon   D. Captain James Cook

4. The word "descendent" in this story means:
   A. relative   B. dead person
   C. bandicoot   D. explorer

5. Many of the first colonists came to Australia because:
   A. They came as tourists and decided to stay.
   B. They were prisoners.
   C. They were born there.
   D. They liked the scenery.

Total Problems: ___   Total Correct: ___   Score: ___

© Carson-Dellosa CD-2206   4

Page 5

Name _____   Pretest

Read each passage. Circle the letter beside the correct answer.

Manicuring and coloring fingernails are certainly not recent beauty practices. Archaeologists excavating at the royal tombs at Ur of the Chaldees in Babylonia discovered a gold manicure set used by someone in the year 3200 B.C. That would make it over five thousand years old.

Ancient queens like Nefertiti and Cleopatra of Egypt, painted their fingernails and toenails different shades of red to make them more beautiful. For hundreds of years, the upper-class women of Spain also used color on their nails. It seems that history's most cultured women have recognized nail care as being important to their beauty and attractiveness. One wonders what Cleopatra and Nefertiti would think about multicolored nails and nail decals and jewels.

1. The best title for this story is:
   A. Beauty Practices in History   **B. Colorful Nails Are Not New**
   C. Cleopatra and Nefertiti   D. Archaeological Discoveries

2. Having one's nails done appears to be a practice that is how old?
   A. 3200 years   **B. over 5000 years**   C. 50 years   D. just a few years

3. How do we know that ancient queens had their nails manicured?
   A. Archaeologists found their nail polish bottles.
   B. Archaeologists found artificial nails in the tombs.
   C. Archaeologists found a gold manicure set in a tomb.
   D. Archaeologists found mummies with manicured nails.

4. Which sentence states an opinion?
   A. Manicuring and coloring fingernails are certainly not recent beauty practices.
   B. That would make it over five thousand years old.
   C. For hundreds of years, the upper-class women of Spain also used color on their nails.
   D. It seems that history's most cultured women have recognized nail care as being important to their beauty and attractiveness.

Saltwater taffy is a popular confection that was developed completely by accident. David Bradley owned a store on the boardwalk in Atlantic City, New Jersey in 1883. His taffy was badly damaged when it got soaked during a storm. A little girl came in the next morning asking for taffy, to which Mr. Bradley disgustedly replied that this was "saltwater taffy." Instead of being disappointed, the little girl thought the "new" candy was delicious, and soon other children wanted some of that wonderful new candy. A bit of advertising and word-of-mouth spread the news. Today, it is estimated that thousands of pounds of saltwater taffy are sold every summer day in Atlantic City, and this delicious accident tantalizes taste buds all over the world.

5. This story is about:
   A. a storm in Atlantic City   B. an accident on the boardwalk
   C. how saltwater taffy was invented   D. why it is important to advertise candy

Total Problems: ___   Total Correct: ___   Score: ___

© Carson-Dellosa CD-2206   5

Page 6

Name _____   Pretest

Read the passage. Circle the letter beside each correct answer.

Obtain a set of four rubber balls of equal size and weight. Begin by throwing just one ball straight up in the air with your right hand and catching it with the same hand. Repeat this several times, throwing the ball about a foot high and as straight as possible. Follow the same procedure with your left hand. When you've conquered that exercise, toss the ball with your right hand, giving it a slight left arch; catch it with your left hand and toss it back to your right. Next take two balls, holding one in each hand. Toss the ball from your right hand, flip the ball from your left hand to your right, catch the ball with your left, and continue the cycle. Work your way up to three, and then four balls.

1. These directions tell you how to:
   A. throw a ball straight   B. catch a baseball
   C. serve a tennis ball   **D. juggle**

2. The first thing you should do, after finding four balls, is:
   A. Toss a ball with your right hand and catch it with your left.
   B. Work your way up to three, and then four balls.
   C. Throw one ball straight up and catch it with the same hand.
   D. Flip the ball.

3. When using two balls, after you toss the ball from your right hand, you should:
   A. Drop the other one.
   B. Flip the ball from your left hand to your right.
   C. Try to hit it with the other ball.
   D. Bounce the ball.

In the following excerpts from restaurant reviews, you will find examples of figurative language. Select the best meaning for the boldfaced expression.

4. Lately, though, the cooking seems to have lost some of its polish; it's **intriguing but uneven.** The cooking is:
   A. interesting but not dependably good
   B. good, but not cooked completely
   C. good, but not served well
   D. interesting, but it doesn't look good

5. This hangout takes wrap-making to a new level of creativity, using tortillas **as colorful as the fillings.** The tortillas are:
   A. not real; this means the paper they are wrapped in
   B. ordinary tortillas
   C. available in different flavors
   D. multicolored

Total Problems: ___   Total Correct: ___   Score: ___

© Carson-Dellosa CD-2206   6

Page 7

Name _____   Pretest

Read the passage. Circle the letter beside each correct answer.

Death Valley Scotty was a rich old man who lived in a castle in Death Valley. Everyone knew he was rich because he would tip waitresses with hundred-dollar bills and throw silver dollars in the street just to watch people scramble for them. No one knew how Scotty got so rich, though. Legend has it that one day Scotty was out in the Panamint Mountains with his favorite mule, Betsy. Betsy was feeling mighty jumpy, and wouldn't do what Scotty wanted her to. Finally, he just let the old mule go where she wanted to. She headed up a narrow gorge. It was late afternoon and hot enough to fry an egg on the sand. Suddenly, she stopped and brayed like she was sick. Scotty scratched his head, and said, "Betsy, I think you've gone just about far enough with this foolishness. We're getting out of here." But Betsy wouldn't budge. She got behind Scotty and pushed him into a dry, rocky ravine. He got up, dusted himself off, said a few choice words to Betsy, and looked around. He couldn't believe his eyes. All around him were quartz rocks, and in the quartz were huge chunks of gold. He climbed out of the ravine and kissed Betsy on the nose. From that day on, she was called Gold-Nosed Betsy.

1. This main idea of this story is:
   A. how Death Valley Scotty became rich   B. why Scotty lived in a castle
   C. living in Death Valley   D. how stubborn mules are

2. Betsy was:
   A. Scotty's wife   B. Scotty's daughter
   C. Scotty's favorite mule   D. Scotty's girlfriend

3. When Scotty said, "Betsy, I think you've gone just about far enough with this foolishness," he was probably feeling:
   A. hungry   B. sleepy
   C. hot, tired, and disgusted   D. worried that Betsy was sick

4. In this story, the word ravine means:
   A. a deep gully   B. a wide river   C. a dark cave   D. an old shack

5. If this story is a legend:
   A. it is factual and true
   B. it is gossip
   C. it was found on a map
   D. it has been passed down from person to person

6. When Scotty said a few choice words to Betsy, he was probably:
   A. telling her how smart she was
   B. telling her to go get help
   C. fussing at her for pushing him in the ravine
   D. crying because he was hurt

Total Problems: ___   Total Correct: ___   Score: ___

© Carson-Dellosa CD-2206   7

© Carson-Dellosa CD-2206

Write the answer to each problem in the correct circle.

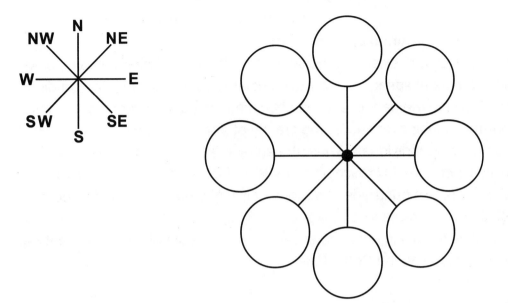

1. In the circle opposite southeast, write the number of pairs of legs on a polar bear.

2. In the east circle, write the number of feet in three yards.

3. In the north circle, write the number of yards that comprise three feet.

4. In the circle between south and west, write the number of nickels in $3.00.

5. In the west circle, write the sum of the numbers in the east and northwest circles.

6. In the southeast circle, write the difference between the numbers in the southwest and north circles.

7. In the south circle, write the answer to "4,518 divided by 9".

8. In the northeast circle, write the answer to "1,760 multiplied by 3."

9. Cross out any number that is less than 5.

10. Add the remaining numbers. Add 1 to the number and then divide by 3.

11. Write the answer in this blank. _____

> Use this space for your work on questions 7, 8, and 10.

Total Problems: _____   Total Correct: _____   Score: _____

Read each passage and question. Circle the letter beside the correct answer.

Animal Life on Earth

Earth teems with life. Living creatures exist from ocean depths to the highest mountain peaks; from equatorial jungles and hot mineral springs to the frozen polar wastelands; from the blinding brightness and aridity of the desert to the dark intestines of animals. In each environment, untold numbers of individual organisms inhabit every nook and cranny of available space. Most animal and plant species contain a myriad of individuals. Thus, the surface layer of most meadow soils contains several million animals per acre. Microscopic animals and plants exist in uncountable numbers. One gram of soil may contain hundreds of millions of living things. Birds and insects exist in populations so large that they create local "plague" conditions. Aquatic life is no less abundant. Certainly, our planet Earth is a thriving environment with the tiniest of animals and creatures living in all places between the Arctic and the South Pole.

1. The main idea of the paragraph is that:
    A. Many living creatures are microscopic and exist in great numbers.
    B. Living creatures exist even in the dark intestines of animals.
    C. The earth has living creatures existing in all kinds of environments.
    D. Meadow soils contain large amounts of animal life.

LDL Cholesterol

One of the more critical components to a person's health is low-density, lipoprotein commonly known as LDL. This component is often referred to as the "bad" cholesterol. When present in high amounts, the small, dense LDL complex has the tendency to deposit itself on the inside of a blood vessel's wall. Because LDL is deposited inside the cells, fatty patches form in the lining of the arteries. Cholesterol that is carried by LDL raises the risk of developing heart disease.

2. The main idea of this paragraph is that:
    A. LDL has a tendency to deposit itself on the inside of a blood vessel's wall.
    B. Lipoprotein is believed to collect cholesterol.
    C. The bad cholesterol is found in men and women over the ages of 40.
    D. LDL is the lipoprotein that raises a person's chance of developing heart disease.

Total Problems:	Total Correct:	Score:

Read each passage and question. Circle the letter beside the correct answer.

Secondhand Smoke

Scientists have found that nonsmokers who live or work with smokers have a higher risk for lung cancer than nonsmokers who do not have this type of exposure. Furthermore, secondhand smoke greatly affects children. Infants of smoking mothers are three times more likely to die of sudden infant death syndrome if the mother chooses to smoke during her pregnancy. Children who are frequently exposed to secondhand smoke are also more likely to get ear infections, pneumonia, bronchitis, tonsillitis, and a number of other health-related problems.

1. The main idea of the passage above is that:
    A. Infants do not seem to be too affected by secondhand smoke.
    B. Nonsmokers who live or work around smokers have an increased risk of developing respiratory problems.
    C. Women who smoke during pregnancy are not harming the unborn infant.
    D. Cigarette smoke contains toxins.

Day Dreaming

Day dreaming is similar to night dreaming in that the mind tries to make sense of random thoughts. The day dream uses images with which one is familiar to form a logical sequence of events. By sitting quietly and letting your daydreams emerge instead of squelching them, you may find that there are parts of yourself to which you have not been listening. According to some psychologists, the day dream plays an important part in organizing and sorting out our lives. The day dream helps to sort out the things one does not understand as well as organize the agendas of the day. However, it is probably not a good idea to day dream in the seventh grade English class, especially if the teacher and class are discussing an important reading or homework assignment.

2. The main idea of the passage above is that:
    A. Day dreams help people to sort out and organize things.
    B. You may find that there is a part of yourself you have not been listening to.
    C. Day dreaming uses images with which we are familiar to form a logical sequence of events.
    D. Night dreaming cannot be compared to day dreaming.

Name _____

Read each passage and question. Circle the letter beside the correct answer.

An *inference* is an assumption based on facts and evidence that are given.

Iridology

Iridology is the study of the iris of the eye. *Iri* and *iris* come from the Greek name of the goddess of the rainbow, Iris. The Greeks named the colored part of the eye after such a goddess because they noticed eyes come in many colors. However, most iridologists agree that there are only two colors of eyes—blue and brown. Brown eyes are traced back to more temperate regions near the equator while historically blue eyes originate from colder regions. Green eyes are the result of mixed races. Iridologists also claim that if a person ate only pure foods and cleared the surroundings of pollutants, the eyes would become more blue.

1. From the passage, one can infer that:
    A. If a person has green or brown eyes, then perhaps he or she is living in a polluted environment or isn't eating enough pure foods.
    B. Brown eyes are traced to more temperate regions near the equator.
    C. Brown is the best color for eyes.
    D. Iridologists only recognize two colors of eyes.

Horses

Historically, the major function of the horse has been in assisting civilizations to conquer land and to expand in size. Because of the animal's incontestable strength and speed, horses have been useful tools on the battlefield. Even before humans could ride horses, they were used in wars to pull chariots. Furthermore, as horses were used more and more on the battlefield, the animals became a symbol of power and a status symbol of the upper class.

Horses also played a great role in the civilization of the western hemisphere. In the sixteenth century, Spanish conquistadors introduced the horse into the Americas. Evidence shows that horses were pivotal in the settlement of the new world. Civilizations that did not have horses were more likely to remain undeveloped and isolated.

2. An inference in the passage above is that:
    A. Horses were useful tools on the battlefield.
    B. Horses were status symbols for the upper class.
    C. Without the horse, the western world would not be as developed as it is today.
    D. With the horse, man has found a source of entertainment.

| Total Problems: | Total Correct: | Score: |

Read each passage and question. Circle the letter beside the correct answer.

Patrick

Upon opening his door, a woman about twenty-five years old dashed past Patrick and into his living room.

"Help me! Please, sir!" she screamed, as she ran back to the door and locked it.

Patrick's mind went blank. Resorting back to his kindness—even in the midst of this horror—he sheltered her and began to speak boldly to her. "What are you doing? Who are you? Why are you in my apartment? What is going on?"

"I haven't the time, sir. Can I stay here for a short while?" she shouted.

Patrick shakily agreed.

1. An inference in the passage above is that:
   - A. The girl has lost her way and needs time to think.
   - B. The girl has lost the keys to her car and is trying to find them.
   - C. The girl is being pursued by someone, and she needs a place to hide for a while.
   - D. The girl's parents are looking for her, and their car is parked in front of his door.

Dreams

Dreamers who are female tend to dream of the two sexes equally and with equal encounters of hostility or friendliness. Unlike males, females normally dream of indoor or familiar settings; they often include conversations. Hostile dreams are more often verbally aggressive rather than physically aggressive. Females notice details, particularly of the other people in the dream. They notice facial features, colors, and other details.

2. An inference one can make from the above passage is that:
   - A. Females normally dream of indoor or familiar settings.
   - B. Males' dreams are often more verbally aggressive.
   - C. Females and males often dream the same kinds of dreams.
   - D. Males are more likely to dream of unfamiliar settings usually set outdoors.

Total Problems:	Total Correct:	Score:

Name _____

Read the passage and answer the questions that follow. Circle the letter beside the correct answer.

Neil

At first Neil didn't realize where he was. Through blurry eyes and a tired little body, the room seemed strange and almost foreign, he thought. From what his senses could reveal, the furniture was stiff and seemed to have a new smell to it. Furthermore, he felt naked, wearing nothing but a long gown, which looked like something his grandmother would wear. As he eased up in the bed, still feeling drowsy, Neil realized where he was and what was going on. He still had the tube in his arm, but it didn't hurt. It was just annoying.

He was in a room by himself. He wasn't afraid, because he was eleven now and almost in middle school. Everyone had told him that his throat would feel this way, but soon he would begin to feel much better. Anyway, this was only the first full day since it happened.

Slightly propped-up on his pillow and still looking around, he saw the door open. She was smiling and wearing a funny-looking uniform with a white cap on her head. She asked him if he needed anything; maybe some ice cream, she suggested. Feeling quite sore, especially in the back of his mouth, Neil thought the ice cream might be soothing. Plus, he was a little hungry. He said he would take some pralines and cream—his favorite ice cream.

As the woman left his room, someone knocked on his door and said his name. He recognized the voices as those of his mom and dad. He tried to say "Come in," loudly, but his voice was weak and his throat was sore. His dad came over and gave him a little tug on the arm—not the one with the tube in it. He and his dad did all sorts of things together. They had planned to camp out this past weekend, but Neil had to come here instead.

Another knock on the door and the woman with the funny-looking cap came in with the ice cream. Boy, did it ever taste good! It felt good going down the back of his throat. His friend Brad had said that this was why they gave you ice cream at times like this. He said it was because you couldn't eat hard foods for a few days, and ice cream would be perfect. Neil thought he could eat ice cream like this for a week, and all he had to do was press the little button and someone would bring it to him.

1. Which event happened first?
   A. He tried to say "Come in," loudly, but his voice was weak and his throat was sore.
   B. Did it ever taste good; plus it felt good going down the back of his throat.
   C. As he eased up in his bed, still feeling drowsy, Neil realized where he was. . .
   D. She was smiling and wearing a funny-looking uniform with a white cap on her head.

2. One can draw what conclusion as to why Neil is in the hospital?
   A. He was playing soccer and had a serious facial injury.
   B. He is in the hospital to have his tonsils removed.
   C. He was in a car accident and was badly injured on the right side of his head.
   D. He was roller blading with Brad, and somehow Brad tripped him.

Total Problems:	Total Correct:	Score:

Read the passage and answer the questions that follow. Circle the letter beside the correct answer.

Brad Samson

Brad Samson was a music teacher who tried very hard to encourage his students. He had one student, Stephanie Adams, whom he thought had the potential to become a great singer. Stephanie had very little self-confidence, and when try-outs for the school musical were scheduled, she decided not to audition.

Brad approached Stephanie five days before the try-outs and asked her why she wasn't auditioning. Her only response was, "I'm just not good enough." Deep down inside, Brad knew that Stephanie wanted to audition, but just didn't have the courage to do it.

Stephanie was in the school choir and a few other school activities, but her real loves were singing and dancing. Every time Brad suggested that Stephanie audition, she would make excuses. One time she said she had to work, and the next time she said she had a major science project due. This continued for about three days, until finally Brad convinced her to try out.

The auditions went very well; many students participated, and Brad was impressed. Everyone was asked to sing, dance, and read selected monologues. The song Stephanie was asked to sing was one she knew, but she was still very nervous and unsure. The dance she performed was simple; she could have done this one with her eyes closed. After the judges turned in their points, Stephanie won by a great majority. She won the lead in the spring musical, just as Brad had predicted. Stephanie was on her way and Brad was very proud of her.

1. Which event happened first?
    A.   The song Stephanie was asked to sing was one she knew.
    B.   Deep down inside, Brad knew Stephanie wanted to audition.
    C.   When musical try-outs were scheduled, Stephanie decided not to audition.
    D.   This continued for about three days, until finally Brad convinced her.

2. Which one of the following events happened last?
    A.   He had one student Stephanie Adams that he really thought had potential.
    B   After the judges turned in their points, Stephanie won by a great majority.
    C.   One time she said she had to work, and the next she said that she had a science project due.
    D.   Her only response was, "I'm just not good enough."

Total Problems:	Total Correct:	Score:

Read the passage and answer the questions on the following page.

Timothy's Adventure

Timothy ran as fast as his little eight-year-old legs could take him. Running through the mud, he knew if he were to stop that it could get him. "What is it?" Timothy thought to himself. He felt he couldn't take one more step, or he would die from exhaustion. He looked to see if it was still there.

He turned and didn't see it, but as he turned to face the other way, he saw something out of the corner of his eye. It was the monster that he feared, a dog-like creature with beady red eyes and long, shaggy fur.

Quickly, he looked for cover, but the only place he could go was the cornfield that belonged to old man Harold Tutwiler. However, looking closer, he noticed on the other side of the cornfield was the remains of a dilapidated barn. He decided to make a run for it. Running as fast as he could through the field, Timothy heard the creature behind him. Almost panicking, he kept his pace, only expecting the worst in the end.

Reaching the barn and immediately trying to lock himself inside, he heard the monster clawing and making bone-chilling noises outside the barn door. He climbed into the barn loft and waited and listened. He sat there for hours, it seemed, but it was only for a few minutes.

"Thank God, I'm safe," Timothy said, in an unsure, quiet exclamation. He spoke too soon because at that moment the creature, panting heavily, broke through the door and glared at him. What was Timothy to do? The creature was blocking the only entrance in the barn; there were no windows or other doors. Stalking his prey with red hot eyes, the monster found Timothy hiding in the hay. In no time, the creature pounced on Timothy and bared his teeth. Timothy felt the creature's saliva dripping onto his face as the monster prepared to sink his teeth into Timothy's flesh.

Just at that moment Timothy awoke to find his dog Sparky, licking his face from one side to the other. Sweaty and relieved, Timothy realized it was only a dream.

Read each question. Circle the letter beside the correct answer.

1. What does the creature look like?
    A.   dog-like creature with beady, black eyes and long, shaggy fur
    B.   dog-like bird with beady red eyes and long, shaggy fur
    C.   dog-like creature with beady, red eyes and short, shaggy fur
    D.   dog-like creature with beady, red eyes and long, shaggy fur

2. Where does Timothy hide to escape the creature?
    A.   a barn
    B.   a house
    C.   a cornfield
    D.   a school

3. In the third paragraph, what is another word that means the same as *dilapidated*?
    A.   dingy red
    B.   broken-down
    C.   renovated
    D.   newly built

4. Who is Sparky?
    A.   the name of the creature
    B.   the name of the horse
    C.   the name of Timothy's dog
    D.   the name of the bird

5. As the creature was about to bite Timothy, what did Timothy feel dripping onto his face?
    A.   blood
    B.   saliva
    C.   water
    D.   corn

6. "Timothy's Adventure" is about a:
    A.   real adventure a young boy had with a mean creature
    B.   real adventure a young boy had while staying with his grandfather
    C.   make-believe story that a young boy created to tell his friends
    D.   bad dream that a young boy had

Total Problems:	Total Correct:	Score:

> *Figurative Language* uses devices such as similes and metaphors to represent something else.
> Examples: *The sky is cloudy and gray.* (Literal Language)
> *The sky is like a gray cat in the fog.* (Figurative Language)

Read the poem and then circle the letter beside each correct answer.

Life

Watching and waiting to fulfill my dreams
I'm lying here wondering
where the road leads.
Years are behind me and still more ahead;
I don't want to waste another
moment here in this bed.
There is so much to do, so much to see,
and a big fence standing in front of me.
I want to leave, and I want to fly,
without taking the time
to even say good-bye.
I'm young and naive
in trust do you not believe?
Let me go; I want to live.
I have so much more to give.

1. In line 8, the word "fence" represents:
   A. a high wooden fence which the narrator cannot get over
   B. the prison to which the narrator has been sent
   C. an obstacle in the narrator's life
   D. a detention home

2. The "road" in line 3, refers to the:
   A. interstate
   B. future
   C. new four-lane road
   D. past

3. " . . . I want to fly" in line 9 is an example of a:
   A. metaphor
   B. pun
   C. personification
   D. simile

4. There is a context clue that suggests that the speaker is actually "here in this bed," line 6. What is the clue?
   A. wondering
   B. watching
   C. dreams
   D. lying

5. Another word for "naive" is:
   A. innocent
   B. indifferent
   C. guilty
   D. restless

Total Problems: _____   Total Correct: _____   Score: _____

Name _____

Read the poem and circle the letter beside each correct answer.

Time Passes

A gust of wind blows,
and another leaf drops.
A baby is born,
and a husband goes off to work.

A young woman says, "I do,"
and a wife says, "Good bye."
Two friends embrace,
as they go their separate ways.

A boy wants to play soccer
and a girl wants to be an astronaut.
One grows up strong,
while the other grows up brave.

Dreams are fulfilled,
and others fade.
Promises are broken,
while commitments are made.

The sun begins to rise,
and a new day starts.
Time keeps passing,
while yesterday parts.

1. Lines 1 and 2 possibly suggest:
   A. a tornado
   B. life and death
   C. a blight is killing the tree
   D. fall is on the way

2. "A baby is born" in line 3 employs the writing technique known as:
   A. simile
   B. metaphor
   C. paradox
   D. alliteration

3. The words "fade" and "made," in lines 14 and 16 are examples of:
   A. rhythm
   B. internal rhyme
   C. end rhyme
   D. alliteration

4. In the last two lines of the poem, "Time keeps passing, while yesterday parts," the meaning of the lines is:
   A. time passes, but yesterday divides into parts
   B. time passes, but yesterday is yet to come
   C. time passes, and yesterday goes away
   D. time passes, but yesterday waits for tomorrow

5. The main idea of the poem is:
   A. dreams
   B. time
   C. nature
   D. love

Read the passage. As you consider the meanings of the italicized words, pay attention to the other words (clues) that surround the italicized words. Choose a word from the word bank that is closest in meaning to each italicized word. Write the correct word in the blank beside the italicized word. Not all words are used. Use a dictionary if necessary.

The Cricket

The lowly cricket is no ordinary insect. Although most insects are *loathed*, the cricket has many friends. For centuries, the Chinese and Japanese have kept crickets as pets in elaborate and *luxurious* cages. Friends of the cricket admire its *melodic* fiddling, the *gratifying* music of a relaxing summer evening. This admiration is not *unanimous*, however. Isaac Stern, a famous violinist, was once momentarily *vanquished* by a tiny competitor. He delayed a concert five minutes while attendants *feverishly* tried to find the tiny fiddler, who was happily *nestled* in a potted palm.

1. *loathed*   _____

2. *luxurious*   _____

3. *melodic*   _____

4. *gratifying*   _____

5. *unanimous*   _____

6. *vanquished*   _____

7. *feverishly*   _____

8. *nestled*   _____

Word Bank			
careless	disliked	of one opinion	pleasant
costly	excitedly	opponents	tuneful
defeated	happily	settled	warlike

Total Problems: _____   Total Correct: _____   Score: _____

Name _____

Read each sentence. As you consider the meanings of the italicized words, pay attention to the other words (clues) that surround the italicized words. Choose a definition to match each italicized word. Write the letter of the correct definition in the blank beside each sentence. Not all definitions are used.

1. _____ An old tree in the front yard was his *haven* from the rest of society.

2. _____ Although Jeremy is *fluent* in Spanish, he is very tongue-tied in German.

3. _____ The lack of laws and leadership brought the country to a state of *anarchy*.

4. _____ Be *wary* in situations such as walking alone on dark streets and swimming at night.

5. _____ If Angie falls from the boat, throw her a life vest or another *buoyant* object.

6. _____ All children can be protected from measles if they get a shot and become *immune*.

7. _____ The *conspiracy* to assassinate President Lincoln was a plan that involved several people.

8. _____ The lively conversation made up for the rather *mediocre* meal at the new restaurant.

9. _____ Be sure to get a *competent* electrician, for one who is unskilled can't fix the wiring.

10. _____ Josh was upset when the cab driver *meandered* around the park, for he had a plane to catch and didn't want to miss it.

Definitions

a. average
b. wandered aimlessly
c. qualified, skilled
d. able to speak effortlessly
e. sentimental
f. cautious
g. refuge or shelter
h. a secret agreement or plot
i. able to float
j. political disorder and confusion
k. good-natured
l. safe or unthreatened by

Total Problems:	Total Correct:	Score:

Read the poem and the passage. Read the questions and circle the letter of the correct answer. Use context clues in order to draw conclusions about the passage.

What are little boys made of?
What are little boys made of?
Snakes and snails and puppy dog tails.
That's what little boys are made of.

What are little girls made of?
What are little girls made of?
Sugar and spice and everything nice.
That's what little girls are made of.

There are some fairy tales and rhymes that portray stereotypical sex or gender roles. Obviously, a child is born a certain sex, but he or she learns to adhere to a label and the pattern that society sets for him or her. Many of these learned influences will continue to exist; however, some of the problem is in literature and can be avoided. Gender stereotypes portray girls as angelic, and boys as rough and athletic.

1. After reading the rhyme above, what conclusion could you draw about boys?
    A. Little boys are made of snakes, snails, and puppy dog tails.
    B. Little boys like repetition.
    C. Little boys dislike sugar and spice.
    D. Little boys are likely to be interested in animals, such as snakes and dogs.

2. How is the rhyme above an example of gender stereotyping in literature?
    A. It says that boys will be boys, and girls will be girls.
    B. It implies that boys are closer to nature, while girls are domestic and refined.
    C. It says that all girls like sweets and candy.
    D. It implies that boys can get away with more than girls.

| Total Problems: | Total Correct: | Score: |

Name _____

Read the passage and answer the questions that follow.

New School and New Friends

When Olga and her family moved into Smithville, Olga was a little nervous. Making friends was not easy for her, and moving into a new town was not exactly how Olga had planned to spend her thirteenth birthday. But she had decided to make the best of the move and go to school the next day, instead of waiting until Monday. Her parents had told her that she could begin on Monday, but since it was only Wednesday and the weekend was close, she decided to go ahead and get the first day out of the way.

As the school day began, everyone was talking about the new Swedish girl that had just moved into town. Also, there was already a rumor going around that it was her birthday this weekend, and everyone wanted to be nice to her. The students in Smithville Middle School were unusually nice to people sometimes, and a large group of students decided to throw her a surprise birthday party at Jonathan Allen's lake house located just outside of town. Jonathan was an eighth grader, but everyone liked him. "I know this is hard on her," Laura Shipp said to Jonathan, "because it was really hard on me when I moved here three years ago." Laura remembered how she felt when she first moved here and wanted to make things easier for Olga.

Laura and her friends devised a plan: they would invite Olga to the lake with them this weekend, where everyone would surprise her with a birthday party.

"I'll find the biggest cake I can," Sherman Fincher said, "but it might be difficult to find one on such a short notice."

Laura added, "Don't worry too much about it. Olga is probably more interested in making friends than having a big cake. I know from my own experience." Chris agreed to bring lots of candy, and all the kids agreed to meet at Jonathan's lake house at 3 o'clock on Saturday afternoon.

Now the only thing left to do was to get Olga to come to the lake. Olga did seem to be a shy person to Laura and her friends, and they wondered if she would accept their invitation. As they approached her on Thursday afternoon, Olga would hardly take her eyes off the floor. "Hi, you're new here, aren't you?" Laura asked.

"Yeah," Olga answered sheepishly.

Laura wondered about their plan now, but she asked her anyway, "Well, we were talking and ... what's your name?"

"Olga," she answered, but continued to stare at the floor.

Laura quickly responded, "Well, Olga, we were talking and were wondering if you would like to come to the lake with us this weekend. It'll be fun."

Olga looked around to make sure that Laura was actually speaking to her directly. Finally, she said, "That sounds like fun."

Laura began to smile and said, "Great. I'll pick you up at 2:30 on Saturday afternoon."

When Laura and Olga arrived at the lake at 3 o'clock on Saturday, everyone was waiting and wearing their swimsuits. Olga didn't know how to swim, and she immediately felt a little uneasy. However, she decided to put that aside and try to have fun anyway. Everyone was swimming and playing in the water, but Olga didn't really want to get into the water just yet.

When they began to notice that Olga was not swimming with them, they got out of the water and gathered around her.

"Well, we knew that it was your birthday, and we have a big surprise for you. Happy Birthday. You do like cake, don't you?" asked Sherman.

"I do, but I'm diabetic. I don't think I can," said Olga, feeling sorry for her new friends. "I'm sorry."

Everyone just looked around at each other. They had tried so hard to make her feel welcome, but everything had turned out wrong. Finally, Laura spoke, "Olga, I'm sorry. We tried to have a nice party for you, but it seems that we have done everything wrong.

Olga just laughed and said, "That's all right. What I really wanted was some new friends at school, and that's what I have. Your friendship means more to me than the cake. Thank you so much."

After that afternoon, Olga and the gang became great friends. Olga's new friends learned an important lesson that day which helped them so much in and out of school.

Read each question. Circle the letter beside the correct answer.

1. What do you suppose is the important lesson that Olga's new friends learned that afternoon?
   A. Be careful when you are swimming in the lake.
   B. Friendship is more important than gifts.
   C. Birthday parties are easy to plan for.
   D. Students from Sweden are more difficult to please than American students.

2. Where was the surprise birthday party held for Olga?
   A. Laura Shipp's house
   B. Sherman Fincher's house
   C. Laura's lake house
   D. Jonathan Allen's lake house

3. Why can't Olga eat her birthday cake?
   A. She has been having some stomach problems lately.
   B. Her doctor insists that Olga is allergic to eggs and flour in cakes.
   C. She ate a big slice of chocolate cake before she attended the party.
   D. She has diabetes and is not supposed to eat the cake.

4. "Olga didn't know how to swim, and she immediately felt a little apprehensive. However, she decided to put that aside and try to have fun anyway." What are the context clues for the meaning of the word "apprehensive"?
   A. didn't know how to swim
   B. she decided to put that
   C. immediately felt
   D. try to have fun

5. Why didn't Olga want to swim in the lake?
   A. She forgot her swimsuit.
   B. Her parents wouldn't allow her to swim with other teenagers.
   C. She didn't know how to swim.
   D. Because she was a diabetic, she wasn't supposed to get into the water.

Read the passage and answer the questions on the following page.

Lucky Ike

Poor Ike. He didn't want much. He only wanted one thing in life—to play soccer. Ahh the money...the awards...the fame he'd have.

"Ike!" Coach Bull's bellowing voice snapped him back to his senses. "It's game time, Ike!"

"Oh yeah!" he replied.

He had forgotten for a moment. Today was the big game. Northwest Middle School was in the state soccer championship. If Ike was ever to shine, today was the day.

Ike sprinted out onto the field in front of the roaring crowd. He neared the middle of the field before he managed to get tangled in his shoelaces and fall flat on his face.

The crowd roared with laughter as Ike trotted toward his reserved spot on the bench. He squeezed in between the coach and the water cooler. He somehow hoped that the coach would notice him here and put him into the game.

By halftime, the game was a tie. During the second half, the broiling June heat had begun to affect both teams. Players became exhausted and then retired to the artificial coolness of the locker room. Soon, Ike found himself almost alone on the bench beside the coach.

"Oh no," sighed Coach Bull as another player collapsed.

"Wow!" thought Ike. "Now Coach has to play me because there is no one else."

"Well, I suppose you're our last hope, Ike," Coach Bull groaned.

Quickly Ike sprinted onto the field, this time keeping his balance. He wasn't in the game over three minutes before everything went into slow motion, just like a movie. The whistle screeched and the play resumed. The ball came to Ike, and he dove.

Pow! Lights flashed like some mad carnival.

Ike awoke to cheers in the hospital room. His team had won. Ike had hit his head on the goal post, and the goalie had laughed so hard that he didn't notice the ball scoot by into the goal.

"Well, I guess I did my part today," Ike said, as he rubbed his head where a goose egg was presently forming.

Read each question. Circle the letter beside the correct answer.

1. One could say the story is mainly about:
    A. a very awkward boy
    B. a mean coach
    C. avoiding heat stroke
    D. always winning

2. Ike wanted to play soccer for all of the following reasons except:
    A. awards
    B. his parents
    C. fame
    D. money

3. An antonym of the word "resume" is:
    A. continue
    B. fail
    C. erupt
    D. stop

4. Coach Bull finally decides to play Ike because:
    A. Ike was the best player on the team.
    B. All the other players had collapsed and were in the locker room.
    C. Ike's parents had persuaded the coach to play Ike.
    D. The team members persuaded the coach to play Ike.

5. "... the artificial coolness of the locker room" is just another way of saying:
    A. The locker room was underground.
    B. The locker room just seemed to be cool.
    C. The locker room had air conditioning.
    D. The locker room had solar panels.

6. "Pow! Lights flashed like some mad carnival." When this happens in the story:
    A. Ike suddenly realizes what he must do, and he kicks the ball.
    B. Lightning strikes the light post on the soccer field.
    C. The soccer ball hits the light post and breaks the light.
    D. Ike hits his head on the goal post and knocks himself unconscious.

Read the passage and answer the questions on the following page.

Anyone Sitting Here?

One day at the movies, my mother embarrassed herself so badly that neither she nor I can ever forget that boisterously entertaining incident. The rain was pouring that day, and the thunder was loud and crashing. She and I thought it was a perfect day for a movie.

After we decided which movie we wanted to see, we dressed and headed for Albertville. The rain seemed to come down harder and faster the closer we came to our destination. Finally, after driving at a much slower speed than usual, we arrived at the theater only to find that we were late.

Disregarding the fact that we had missed five minutes of the opening scene, we purchased tickets and went into the theater. Finding a seat in a dark theater is always a difficult task, but we were anxious to get settled because we really wanted to see this show. Our eyes had not quite adjusted to the darkness, but I tried to follow my mother as she somewhat blindly looked for two seats.

She went to the middle of the theater and began to move down a row where she thought there were two empty seats. The next thing that I saw, however dark, was the figure of my mother sitting down, right into a spot where there was no seat. For whatever reason, the seat had been removed. So instead of sitting down into a seat, my mom was sprawled on the floor. Trying to maintain herself, my mom whispered loudly, "Hope, help me. I can't get up." It seemed that one of her legs had managed to get caught under the seat in front of her, and she was tugging and sighing as she tried to free it, while I giggled without restraint at the predicament my mom was in. After a minute, it seemed, my mom was free and standing, and fortunately the lights were out, because she was terribly embarrassed.

My mother and I finally located two empty seats about four rows back and proceeded to watch the movie, amidst a few silent giggles and whispers. On the way home that afternoon, my mother made me promise not to tell Dad about her disconcerting adventure that day. I did keep the promise for one hour, but it was just too funny not to tell.

Read each question. Circle the letter beside the correct answer.

1. Where did the story take place?
   A. beach
   B. city
   C. theater
   D. school

2. What is the funny incident that happened in the story?
   A. The mother only wore one earring and two different colored shoes.
   B. The narrator's mother missed her chair and sat on the floor.
   C. The mother fell out of her seat onto the floor.
   D. By mistake the mother sat down into a space where a seat had been removed.

3. What did the mother make the narrator promise?
   A. not to tell the narrator's dad about the incident
   B. not to tell anyone about the incident
   C. not to tell the narrator's dad they went to Albertville
   D. not to tell the doctor they had left the house

4. In the last paragraph, another word for "disconcerting" is:
   A. flirtatious
   B. embarrassing
   C. musical
   D. serious

5. Number the phrases from the passage in sequential order.

A. _____ . . . we were anxious to get settled because we really wanted to see this show.

B. _____ . . . the thunder was loud and crashing.

C. _____ Our eyes had not quite adjusted to the darkness, as I tried to follow . . .

D. _____ The rain seemed to come down harder and faster . . .

E. _____ . . . my mother made me promise not to tell Dad . . .

F. _____ Trying to maintain herself, my mom whispered loudly, "Hope, help me."

Read the passage and answer the questions on the following page.

A Funny Sight

The weather report for that humid July summer night wasn't that kind, but we had been planning this trip for a long time. So we decided to go ahead with our camping trip. My big brother Scott and I had chosen a perfect spot on the side of the mountain, not thinking that if it did storm, we might get drenched.

Scott had settled on his air mattress, and I was on my sleeping bag. Both of us were fast asleep when the fun began. We had been sleeping maybe about one hour when we were awakened by the storm. I said, "Scott, listen to that storm. I bet it's gonna be a gully washer. It's a good thing we dug that drainage ditch around the tent."

"Jay, we'll be fine. Go back to sleep," Scott said assuringly. My big brother was in the twelfth grade, and everyone liked him, especially me. In many ways, he was my hero, and I would do anything for him, and he would do the same for me.

About thirty minutes later, the rain was falling in torrents, and the tent was rocking, while the trees cracked and groaned in the wind. I couldn't sleep; all I could do was lie there and listen. Looking and feeling around with my small flashlight, I yelled, "Scott, there is water coming in our tent." At first, he didn't appear to hear me, so I nudged him and repeated it.

This time Scott jumped up and unzipped the tent and hurried outside. He had his floodlight with him and both of us could see our immediate area. It was then that I noticed that there was a big puddle of water beginning to form in our tent. As I pulled back the flap of the tent, I saw one of the funniest sights I have seen in a while. My brother in his purple-leopard boxer shorts was busy digging frantically around the drainage ditch with an old army shovel that our dad had given us. The sight of him standing there with rain pouring all over him and yelling for me to come out and help him made me laugh out loud. I couldn't stop laughing as I stumbled out to help him.

After some time we widened and cleared the drainage ditch around our tent, but the water inside the tent was another story. My sleeping bag was soaking wet, and Scott's air mattress was floating by now. Even Scott laughed when he saw this.

We grabbed our things and decided to move around the mountain to a pavilion that we had seen earlier that afternoon on our trek up the mountain. We thought we could sleep on the picnic table that was under the pavilion.

As we once again settled down to try to get some sleep, Scott developed a thirst for a soda, so both of us decided to get up and have sodas. We ended up talking and drinking sodas for the rest of the night, probably until around 5 o'clock in the morning. But that was great with me, because I always like hanging out with my big brother.

Read each question. Circle the letter beside the correct answer.

1. The following statements about the weather are false except which one?
   A. The day had been humid, but no one suspected any bad weather.
   B. It was a typical summer night, and they were sure the weather would be good.
   C. It was raining very hard before they left their home that day.
   D. Scott and Jay knew that the weather might be bad before they left home.

2. The "funny sight" mentioned in the story was:
   A. Jay digging around in the rain in his purple-leopard boxer shorts.
   B. Scott running around in the rain in his paisley-leopard boxer shorts.
   C. Scott digging around in the rain in his purple-leopard boxer shorts.
   D. the rain coming in the tent and soaking everything Jay and Scott took with them

3. A word that means the same as "trek" is:
   A. tricked
   B. hike
   C. picnic
   D. quarrel

4. Which one of the following events happened first in the story?
   A. . . . Scott jumped up and unzipped the tent and hurried outside.
   B. We ended up talking and drinking sodas for the rest of the night . . .
   C. Both of us were fast asleep when the fun began.
   D. Looking and feeling around with my small flashlight, I yelled, . . .

5. The expression "gully washer" means:
   A. a lot of rain
   B. a part on cars to wash the windshields
   C. to dig a drain
   D. a light rain

6. Scott and Jay did all the following during the night except:
   A. They did get some sleep before the onslaught of the rain.
   B. Scott used his flashlight, but Jay didn't have a light to use.
   C. They talked and drank sodas during a big part of the night.
   D. They dug a drain around the tent before they went to sleep.

7. Another word for "pavilion" is:
   A. truck   B. mall
   C. umbrella   D. shelter

Read the passage and answer the questions on the following page.

The Best Christmas

Sheila slowly glanced around the dull hospital room. A large green wreath hung on the door. Numerous Christmas cards were displayed on the two bedside tables.

"Mommy?" Jacob's tiny voice squeaked.

"Yes, dear?" Sheila asked, as she walked to the bed where her seven-year-old son lay.

"I finished my letter to Santa," Jacob stated with excitement. He then proudly held it up for his mother to see.

"You've done a great job, Jacob," Sheila responded, as she silently read Jacob's letter. The letter read: *Dear Santa, All I want for Christmas is to get better and go home. I have been good. Thanks, Jacob*

Sheila blinked back the tears as she handed the letter back to her son. It hurt her so much to see him suffering this way. "You know, Jacob, sometimes Santa isn't able to bring us everything we want," she tried to explain without being so pessimistic.

"Yes, I know, Mom, but I've been really good this year," he replied with such confidence.

"That's true," his mother agreed. It seemed as though Jacob had been too sick and weak to misbehave. Suddenly, a knock was heard on the door and Dr. Clarke, the hospital's neurologist, entered the room without waiting for a response. "Hi there, Jacob," he said with a kind and sincere tone. "How have you been feeling?"

"A lot better," Jacob answered with a smile.

"Good, good fellow," Dr. Clarke replied, while listening to Jacob's heart with his stethoscope. He then turned to Sheila and said, "May I see you in the hall for a minute?"

"Sure," Sheila replied apprehensively. The two exited the room and Jacob continued to read and look at his letter.

"Mrs. Lang," the doctor began, "the results from Jacob's last biopsy have come back." Sheila's face froze and she was speechless. "The tests show that the tumor has completely disappeared, and there are no signs of cancerous cells in any of the surrounding areas. It looks as if the chemo-therapy has worked. The disease is in remission." We will need to check him again in a month to make sure the tumor doesn't return but it should be okay for him to go home for the holidays."

Sheila hardly knew what to do. Should she cry or should she laugh for joy? After all this time, she couldn't believe that Jacob's cancer was finally gone. A rush of happiness flooded her body. Then, she spoke, "Thank you, Dr. Clarke. Thank you so very much."

"I am pleased to give this information to you," the doctor replied. "We can have a meeting with the staff in the next two days and discuss Jacob's outpatient care plan. But, for now, why don't you go in and tell him the good news."

"Okay, I will," Sheila responded with a happiness she had never felt in her life. "Thank you again, Dr. Clarke. You don't know how much this means to Jacob and our family."

Sheila opened the door to her son's hospital room and entered. She couldn't wait to tell Jacob the good news that his Christmas wish was going to come true after all.

Read each question. Circle the letter beside the correct answer.

1. The main idea of this story is:
   A.   There are good doctors everywhere.
   B.   Spending the holiday in a hospital would be pleasant.
   C.   Sometimes wishes come true.
   D.   A parent cannot be taken for granted.

2. What did Jacob want for Christmas?
   A.   a new computer
   B.   to get better and go home
   C.   a private room
   D.   a new doctor

3. "The tests show that the tumor has completely disappeared, and there are no signs of can-cerous cells in any of the surrounding areas. It looks as if the chemotherapy has worked. The disease is in remission." Which is _not_ a context clue for the meaning of the word remission?
   A.   the tumor has completely disappeared,
   B.   there are no signs of cancerous cells
   C.   any of the surrounding areas
   D.   the chemotherapy has worked

4. "You know, Jacob, sometimes Santa isn't able to bring us everything we want," she tried to explain without being so pessimistic. What inference can be made by Sheila's comment to her son Jacob?
   A.   She is trying to prepare her son for disappointment in case he does not get better and cannot go home.
   B.   She is trying to tell Jacob there is no Santa Claus.
   C.   She is trying to tell Jacob that their family does not have much money.
   D.   She is trying to tell Jacob that he wants too much.

5. Another word or expression that means the same as "remission" is:
   A.   coma
   B.   free from symptoms
   C.   terminally ill
   D.   anxiety

6. Which event happened last?
   A.   He then proudly held it up for this mother to see.
   B.   A rush of happiness flooded her body.
   C.   Sheila told Dr. Clarke, "You don't know how much this means to Jacob and our family."
   D.   "Hi there, Jacob," he said with a kind and sincere tone.

Read the passage and answer the questions on the following page.

Swimming with Nurse Sharks

This summer my dad and I shared an experience that I will never forget. We went scuba diving in the crystal blue waters of the Gulf of Mexico. My mom and brother missed this exploration because my brother had a golf tournament in Birmingham. My mom decided to accompany Brax to the tournament, so my vacation became a father-daughter one. Saddened that this would not be another memorable family vacation, I was still excited about my first saltwater dive, and being able to share this experience with my dad only made it more special.

The boat was rocking and my nerves were running wild as we approached the oil rig. Then, suddenly, I became sick. One of the crew members tried to calm my nerves while the other one told my dad that I was sick. No matter what the crew members did to make me feel better, nothing helped as much as a hug from my dad. I spent the rest of the ride asleep with my head on my dad's shoulder. Just knowing that my dad is always there gives me the safest feeling in the world.

Once the boat stopped, my dad's main concern was to get me into the water. As I was getting dressed, everywhere I turned my dad was there holding whatever I needed. I entered the water and waited for him. Once my dad and the dive master joined me, we began our descent. Not long after we began our descent, the dive master stopped me. Wondering why the descent had stopped, I looked around and realized that my dad was not with us. My heart started to race as I looked around for him. He was nowhere to be found. Finally, I looked up and saw two legs kicking at the surface. Lacking the proper amount of weight, he was stranded at the surface. The dive master ascended and grabbed Dad's hand and pulled him down.

Once we finished our descent, we were ready to explore. I had never realized how vast the ocean was until I was really in it. I felt a little insignificant, like a grain of sand in the Sahara Desert. However, knowing that my dad was there with me made this feeling go away. We had been swimming around at a depth of sixty feet for about fifteen minutes when dad informed me that he was low on air. He returned to the surface. With a sufficient air supply, the dive master and I decided to continue our dive at twenty feet.

Swimming around the oil rig, I saw a mysterious dark figure in the distance. Swimming closer, I struggled to make out the shapes: a long, light brown tail and a dorsal fin. Then it moved and I noticed it was a shark. My heart started to pound, as I realized that four or five sharks surrounded me. Meticulously studying the sharks, I realized they were only nurse sharks and practically harmless. I swam around to get a closer look at one of the shark's faces. It had a kind, yet mysterious, look in its eyes. I failed to see how someone could perceive this to be a life-threatening animal.

I hated to call this perfect dive to a halt, but my air supply was running low. Seeing a shark on my first saltwater dive was an experience that I will never forget. I couldn't wait to tell my mom and brother about this unbelievable experience. I wished this could have been another one of our unforgettable family vacations, but my brother placed in the golf tournament so the separation was worthwhile this time. Furthermore, scuba diving in the Gulf of Mexico was the best father-daughter vacation I could have ever imagined.

Read each question. Circle the letter beside the correct answer.

1. The story is mainly about:
    A. snorkeling in the Gulf of Mexico
    B. swimming with nurse sharks in the Gulf of Mexico
    C. a family of four who enjoy a vacation together in the Gulf of Mexico
    D. sharing a special vacation experience with a dad

2. In the fourth paragraph, the narrator compares herself to a grain of sand in the Sahara Desert. This comparison between the narrator and sand is called a:
    A. metaphor
    B. simile
    C. pun
    D. paradox

3. Another word or expression that means the same as meticulously is:
    A. approximately
    B. carefully
    C. not precisely
    D. haphazardly

4. Why didn't the narrator's brother go scuba diving?
    A. He preferred to sun on the beach instead.
    B. He went deep-sea fishing with his mother.
    C. He attended a golf tournament in Birmingham.
    D. He stayed home to study for a summer school exam.

5. Upon their initial descent into the water, the dad becomes stranded because:
    A. He was scared and didn't want to go any further.
    B. Suddenly he was sick and fatigued.
    C. He lacked the proper amount of weight.
    D. He saw a shark in the distance.

6. What happened last in the story?
    A. The boat was rocking and my nerves were running wild as we approached the oil rig.
    B. Swimming around the oil rig, I saw a mysterious dark figure in the distance.
    C. The divemaster ascended and grabbed Dad's hand and pulled him down.
    D. . . . my brother placed in the golf tournament so the separation was worthwhile . . .

| Total Problems: | Total Correct: | Score: |

Read the passage and answer the questions on the following page.

The Last Game

It was the beginning of the end. The final football game had just begun. As a senior, Michelle Rogers was cheering her last football game. She was so excited, but yet so sad. Her cheering career would be over in four quarters.

All the cheerleaders, including Michelle, were lined up ready to cheer the team. This game was not only the last game of the year but also the most important game. Michelle's team, the Greenwood Knights, were facing the undefeated Gunter Wild-cats. The teams were lined up, ready to run onto the field. The band started playing and both teams ran out. The fans were ecstatic!

The kickoff was about to begin. Michelle was so excited. The kick was absolutely the greatest, and the fans went crazy. The announcer was talking about all the fans and the excitement of the game. Led by Michelle, the cheerleaders had a great cheer at all times.

Suddenly, it was already halftime, and the score was 14-7, with Gunter leading. Michelle wanted her Knights to win. Her voice was almost gone from cheering her team on for the first half of the game. The second half would be even worse because the score was so close.

When the second half started, both teams were really excited. Michelle wondered what the coach could have said to the players in the locker room. After cheering long and hard, it was finally down to the last quarter with one minute to go, and the score was 14-14.

Michelle was ecstatic! Greenwood had the ball at the 50-yard line. For a second, she wandered away in her own world—thinking about her past football games. Suddenly, she was awakened from her momentary daydreaming by a friend scream-ing at her that they had won the game. The crowd was going crazy.

As Michelle joined the crowd's spirit and vivacity, she again flashed back through four years of fun games and sportsmanship. She remembered the winning games, and she also remembered the losing games. However, she would always remember this night because it seemed a perfect ending to a perfect season.

Read each question. Circle the letter beside the correct answer.

1. One main idea of this story is:
   A. The Gunter Wildcats always beat the Greenwood Knights.
   B. Michelle Rogers was cheering her last football game.
   C. Sports events can be exciting and provide a lot of great memories.
   D. Baseball is a very tough sport.

2. At halftime, who was winning the game?
   A. Michelle
   B. Gunter
   C. Greenwood
   D. Stewart

3. Which one of the following events occurred last?
   A. As Michelle joined the crowd's spirit and vivacity, she again flashed . . .
   B. . . . she was awakened from her momentary daydreaming by a friend . . .
   C. . . . it was down to the last quarter with one minute to go, . . .
   D. The teams were lined up ready to begin their game.

4. Another word that means the same as the word "ecstatic" is:
   A. overwhelmed
   B. unruly
   C. angry
   D. moody

5. Michelle was awakened from her daydreaming by:
   A. the loud noise of the crowd, jumping and screaming
   B. a friend screaming at her
   C. her mother screaming that breakfast was ready
   D. her teacher telling her to wake up and do her work

6. Which one of the following statements is not true?
   A. Tonight was the last game of the season.
   B. At halftime, Greenwood was losing the game.
   C. Gunter had only lost one game this year prior to the game with Greenwood.
   D. Gunter lost the game with Greenwood.

7. A word that has the opposite meaning of the word "vivacity" is:
   A. happiness   B. sensitivity
   C. inanimate   D. joy

Total Problems:	Total Correct:	Score:

Read the following passage and answer the questions on the following page.

Good Business Sense

Brad slowly sipped his scalding coffee as he watched the glossy California sun come up over the seemingly never-ending Pacific Ocean. Brad Stewart was about to embark on one of the most important and most memorable days of his life. Today was the grand opening of Brad's new business. He had graduated last year from the University of Southern California with a degree in business.

The plan for Stewart's Software Company had been in the making for almost a year now. While Brad had been working with a larger company, he had been gathering information for what was needed to create and manage a new, up-and-coming business. A building had already been purchased 34 days ago and had been renovated with offices, warehouse, and retail floor space. Loans had been made from the bank as well as from Brad's parents. Finally, the day had arrived.

The store was set to make its opening at eight o'clock. Brad was there early enough to make sure everything went smoothly. By the time the doors were open, several customers were waiting in line to enter. At eight o'clock sharp when Brad unlocked the automatic door and stepped in front of it to open, nothing happened. The same thing had happened with the door the day before, but Brad knew exactly what to do. Quickly he ran upstairs, adjusted the automatic electric eye switch, and then rushed back downstairs. He waved to the customers outside and stepped again in front of the door. It worked and the people rushed in as kids would to the grand opening of a new toy store. It seemed as if not one customer left the store empty-handed. The first day didn't seem to have enough hours before the closing hour of five o'clock. Brad's smile seemed to stay intact throughout the day and seemed to get even larger as he calculated the business from the first day.

The first day's income was enough to make a substantial dent in Brad's loans. Moreover, he was able to make his loans disappear within the first three months of business. Now, three years later, Brad runs a large chain of stores in northern California and is considered one of the most successful businessmen in the state.

Read each question. Circle the letter beside the correct answer.

1. What happened on the day the store was set to open?
   A. The grand opening of a new toy store took place.
   B. Brad opened the door at eight o'clock sharp to greet the customers.
   C. The automatic door would not open.
   D. Brad graduated from the University of Southern California.

2. Another word that means the same as intact is:
   A. covered
   B. whole
   C. twisted
   D. broken

3. How much money did Brad make the first day his store opened?
   A. enough money to pay off much of his debt
   B. not much money at all
   C. enough money to pay off all of his debt
   D. no money at all

4. The setting for "Good Business Sense" is:
   A. southern California
   B. Pacific Ocean
   C. northern California
   D. Oregon

5. Brad graduated with a degree in:
   A. English
   B. law
   C. mathematics
   D. business

6. A word that means the opposite of the word "substantial" is:
   A. above
   B. insignificant
   C. underground
   D. great

7. One might decide the main idea of the story is:
   A. to always make sure the door is working properly before scheduling a grand opening
   B. that everyone should graduate from a university or college
   C. that one should never make loans from a bank or lending institution
   D. that with hard work and perseverance a person can become successful

Total Problems:	Total Correct:	Score:

Read the passage and answer the questions that follow. Circle the letter beside the correct answer.

Angel's Punishment

As he was coming down for breakfast, young Angel tripped and bruised his knee. As if this were not bad enough, he had also forgotten to do his book report that was due today in seventh grade English. When his mother asked him if he had finished his report, he said that he had, but she could not see it because he had saved it onto a disk.

Arriving at school, Angel's stomach had more butterflies than a field in early spring. He desperately wanted to get some sort of grade so he thought that if he told his teacher a little white lie he might make something positive out of the situation. When his teacher asked him for his report, he told her that while he was finishing his report, his computer crashed. He begged his teacher for one more day to get it to her. Since Angel had always been a satisfactory student, she decided to allow him another day to get the report to her. After this encounter, the rest of school that day was good.

When the last bell rang for school to end, Angel hurried home to get an early start on his report. Before he was ten feet into his room, his mother called him into the kitchen. She wanted to know what grade he had gotten on his report. He told her that the reports had not been graded yet. When she heard this, his mother became very upset. She said the teacher had called to say how sorry she felt that Angel's computer had crashed and that she was allowing him to turn in the report tomorrow. Angel's stomach hit the floor. With his desperate lies, he had put himself into a web of tangled stories.

After the whole truth was revealed, Angel finished his report on paper, because his computer had been taken away for one week. The report was ten pages handwritten, and it took him three hours to do it, whereas on his computer he could have done it in half the time.

1. The main idea of this story is:
    A.   Doing homework on the computer is simpler than writing it by hand.
    B.   It is all right to stretch the truth just a little.
    C.   It is not so bad to put off doing assignments until the last minute.
    D.   It is always best to tell the truth.

2. In the second paragraph, the expression "Angel's stomach had more butterflies than a field in early spring" means:
    A.   Angel ate some bad food for breakfast.
    B.   Angel is very nervous about the report.
    C.   Angel probably has had a stomach operation recently.
    D.   Angel saw butterflies in a field on his way to school.

| Total Problems: | Total Correct: | Score: |

Name _____

Read the passage and answer the questions that follow. Fill in each blank with the correct answer.

Prague: City of a Hundred Spires

Prague, the capital and largest city of the Czech Republic, lies on both sides of the banks of the Vltava River. Because of its many Gothic churches, it has been called the "City of a Hundred Spires." The city is still recovering from communism, which was expelled in 1989 during the Velvet Revolution. Student protests and marches started the anti-communist revolt that led to the entire city supporting the students' cause.

The Old Town, which served as the seat of government for hundreds of years, lies on the right bank of the Vltava River. Here one can see the Tyn Church and the prestigious Charles University, the oldest in central Europe. The university was established by Charles IV of Bohemia, who was responsible for Prague's "Golden Era," which made the city a cultural and economic center.

Atop the highest point and overlooking the city on the left bank of the Vltava River is Prague Castle, the official residence of the president. The castle has been reconstructed many times throughout history. Its well-known Gothic spires and medieval style were the ideas of Charles IV.

Despite gradual modernization, Old Prague has retained much of its original charm and appearance, with narrow streets and many historic buildings in the Gothic style. Palaces of the old nobility now house government offices and embassies. Prague suffered little damage in World War II and has approximately 1,700 officially designated historic monuments. Prague still remains a picturesque and richly historic city.

1. On the left bank, atop the highest point, is _____, the official residence of the president.

2. Prague lies on both sides of the banks of the _____ River.

3. _____ established the oldest university in central Europe and made the city a cultural and economic center.

4. Because of its many _____ churches, Prague has been called the "City of a Hundred Spires."

5. Prague is still recovering from communism, which was expelled in _____. (year)

Read the passage and answer the questions that follow. Fill in each blank with the correct answer.

Bangkok: "The City of Angels"

Bangkok, the capital and chief port of Thailand, is one of the most important cities in Southeast Asia. It is located on the east bank of the Chao Phraya River, which runs through the city, and is called Krung Thep, or "City of Angels," by the Thai people. Perhaps this modern city's most distinctive features are the approximately 400 Buddhist temples, called "wats." Nearly all of Thailand's citizens are Buddhist.

In smaller villages, many Thai people still live traditionally near the river. The Thai people build wooden houses that stand on stilts in the water. Boats service the houses along the way—bus boats, mail boats, and even ice cream boats stop at the houses which are entered on long, wooden planks. Although Bangkok still has many of these canal dwellings, most people in the city now live in modern apartment buildings.

Although Thai customs and etiquette have generally developed in Western fashion, take note of the following. When traveling in Thailand: (1) Avoid discussing the heads of state and the royal family in a manner that might be interpreted as demeaning or condescending. Thai have a deep love and respect for their monarch. (2) Show respect toward temples, wats and shrines, and all Buddhist images. Women must neither sit next to nor touch a monk. If a female has to hand a monk something, she should pass it to a man to hand to the monk, or place the object on a table or on the floor. (3) The head is the highest and most respected, sacred part of the body; the foot is the lowest. Do not touch a Thai on the head. Do not sit with your feet pointed at a Thai; this is a show of gross disrespect. Do not even use your feet to point at an object, such as luggage. When entering a Thai home or a temple, remove your shoes. Never lose your temper—you will lose the respect and goodwill of all watching.

1. There are nearly 400 Buddhist temples, called _____, in Bangkok.

2. The Thai people have a deep love and respect for their _____.

3. What is the meaning of *Krung Thep*? _____.

4. The _____ River, located on the east bank, flows through Bangkok.

5. It is customary among Thai that women must neither sit next to nor touch a _____.

Total Problems:	Total Correct:	Score:

© Carson-Dellosa CD-2206

Read the passage and answer the questions that follow. Circle the letter beside the correct answer.

Cape Town, South Africa

Cape Town, first called Cape of Good Hope, is the legislative capital and the largest and most scenic city of South Africa. Situated on Table Bay at the foot of Table Mountain, a national landmark, and overlooking the Atlantic Ocean, Cape Town was colonized by European settlers. Its climate is typically Mediterranean—winters are cool and wet, and summers are warm and dry.

Cape Town was founded in 1652 by Jan van Riebeeck to serve as a supply station for the Dutch East India Company. In 1795 it was captured by a British force, but was returned to the Dutch by the Treaty of Amiens in 1803. In 1806 it again came under British control. Following the discovery of diamonds in 1867 and gold in 1886 in the interior, Cape Town became one of the country's largest ports and rail terminals. The Europeans of South Africa created the apartheid policy to assure that they, not the South African non-whites, would have continued economic and social control. In 1991 the laws of apartheid were abolished. In 1994, Nelson Mandela was elected the first democratic president of South Africa.

The city center focuses on the Public Gardens, a remnant of the original settlement, and on the Houses of Parliament. The Castle, begun in 1666 and completed in 1677, was a seat of government in the 17th century, and is now a museum. Cape Town is the headquarters of several banks and insurance companies, and has theaters, museums, and an orchestra. It has two universities: the University of the Western Cape and the University of Cape Town. With so many attractions, it is no wonder that Cape Town continues to be a popular tourist site.

1. Cape Town was founded in 1652 to serve as the:
    A.   national landmark
    B.   supply station for the Dutch East India Company
    C.   headquarters for several banks
    D.   country's largest port and rail terminal

2. The Europeans of South Africa created the apartheid policy. Apartheid means:
    A.   social and economic discrimination against non-whites
    B.   social and economic discrimination against whites
    C.   the discovery of diamonds and gold in South Africa
    D.   the control over ports and railways in South Africa

3. In 1994, who was elected as the democratic president of South Africa?
    A.   Jan van Riebeeck
    B.   Mandela Amiens
    C.   Nelson Hope
    D.   Nelson Mandela

Total Problems:	Total Correct:	Score:

Read the passage and answer the questions that follow. Circle the letter beside the correct answer.

Albert Einstein: Person of the Century

The German-American physicist, Albert Einstein, contributed more than any other scientist to the 20th-century vision of physical reality. Following World War I, his theories—especially his theory of relativity—seemed to point to a pure quality of human thought. The theory is written in the formula $E = mc^2$, which shows how space, time, and gravity are related. The E stands for energy; the m stands for mass; the c^2 stands for the velocity of light, squared.

Einstein's parents, who were Jewish, moved from Ulm to Munich, Germany when Einstein was an infant. The family business was the manufacturing of electrical apparatus. When the business failed in 1894, the family moved to Milan, Italy. At this time, Einstein decided officially to relinquish his German citizenship.

He spent the next years in Europe. He wrote academic papers and held various positions which included: a post at the Swiss patent office in Bern, where he completed an astonishing range of publications in theoretical physics; lecturer at the University of Bern; associate professor of physics at the University of Zurich; professorships at the German University of Prague and at the Zurich Polytechnic; and cross-appointment at the University of Berlin.

The Nobel Prize was awarded to Einstein in 1921 for his work on the photoelectric effect, which explains the absorption and release of energy by certain atoms by incandescent bodies. Einstein remained on the staff of the University of Berlin until 1933. With the rise of fascism in Germany, Einstein moved to the United States in 1933, where he held an analogous research position at the Institute for Advanced Study in Princeton, New Jersey. In 1939, Einstein sent the famous letter to President Franklin D. Roosevelt that urged the United States to develop an atomic bomb before Germany. However, Einstein was a strong advocate of world peace. Because of his many scientific contributions, *TIME* magazine has honored Albert Einstein as the Person of the Century. Einstein died in 1955.

1. What is the name of Einstein's famous theory?
    - A. Theory of Physical Reality
    - B. Theory of Physics
    - C. Theory of Human Thought
    - D. Theory of Relativity

2. In what country was Einstein born?
    - A. United States
    - B. Israel
    - C. Germany
    - D. Switzerland

3. Einstein won the Nobel Prize in 1921 for his work on:
    - A. The Theory of Relativity
    - B. The Photoelectric Effect
    - C. Human Thought
    - D. Physical Reality

Total Problems:	Total Correct:	Score:

Read the passage and answer the questions that follow. Circle the letter beside the correct answer.

Meet the Writer: Mildred D. Taylor

Born in Jackson, Mississippi, Mildred D. Taylor was educated in Toledo, Ohio. She wanted to be a cheerleader in high school but instead was an honor student, a newspaper editor, and a class officer. Every summer Mildred and her family visited Mississippi relatives, and she listened to their stories. By the time she was nine, Mildred knew that she wanted to be a writer. Ms. Taylor attended the University of Toledo and received her Master's degree at the University of Colorado School of Journalism.

Mildred Taylor began her career with the Peace Corps as an English and history teacher in Ethiopia for two years. Later she returned to the United States and was a Peace Corps recruiter. After the Peace Corps, Ms. Taylor became a study skills coordinator for the University of Colorado's Black Education Program.

In 1975, her first novel, *Song of the Trees*, introduced the Logan family to American readers and won first prize in the African-American category in a competition of children's books. *Roll of Thunder, Hear My Cry*, told by Cassie, the first person narrator, was Ms. Taylor's second novel, which won the Newberry Medal in 1977. Published in 1982, *Let the Circle Be Unbroken* continues the Logan story when Cassie is 11 and Stacey is 14. There are two additional short stories about the Logans: "Mississippi Bridge" (1987) and "The Friendship" (1990).

It is quite apparent that Ms. Taylor uses her own early life as the inspiration for her stories. In 1977, when she accepted the Newberry Award for *Roll of Thunder, Hear My Cry*, she talked about her father, who taught her a truer history of black people in the United States than she had learned in school. In all her novels, Mildred D. Taylor pulls her reader into the circle of an inspiring black family.

1. Mildred D. Taylor has written all of the following except:
   A. *Roll of Thunder, Hear My Cry*
   B. *Song of the South*
   C. *Let the Circle Be Unbroken*
   D. "Mississippi Bridge"

2. When Mildred was only nine, she wanted to become a:
   A. teacher
   B. lecturer
   C. writer
   D. nurse

3. In 1977, Ms. Taylor accepted the Newberry Medal for having written:
   A. "The Friendship"
   B. *Let the Circle Be Unbroken*
   C. *Song of the Trees*
   D. *Roll of Thunder, Hear My Cry*

Total Problems:	Total Correct:	Score:

45

Read the passage and answer the questions that follow. Circle the letter beside the correct answer.

Edgar Allan Poe, The Father of Modern Mystery

Edgar Allan Poe was one of America's greatest poets, short-story writers, and literary critics. Poe's parents were touring actors, and both died before he was three years old. He was taken into the home of John Allan, a prosperous merchant in Richmond, Virginia. His early childhood was uneventful, although he studied for 5 years in England.

"The Raven" is Poe's best-known poem and one of the most famous works in American literature. The theme of "The Raven"—the narrator's grief over the loss of an ideal love—recurs in other works by Poe. "To Helen," "Ulalume," and "For Annie" also dramatize deep-felt loyalty to a woman who symbolizes an ideal spiritual value. These poems are noted for their subtle use of rhyme, rhythm, and symbols.

With "The Murders in Rue Morgue" and other short stories, Poe became the father of modern mystery and detective fiction. In "Sonnet to Science" and "The Valley of Unrest," Poe described man's loss of innocence and sense of wonder and beauty. In "Lenore," "Annabel Lee," and "Eldorado," he implies that only love, beauty, or aspiration can save man from despair.

Poe's most popular tales are filled with an atmosphere of the strange, the bizarre, and the terrible. Many of Poe's stories are called "moral allegories" because the theme of moral responsibility prevails in them. Perhaps Poe's best story, "The Fall of the House of Usher," deals with this theme.

Poe earned only a meager living from his writings. Still, during his short life he wrote poems and stories that have made him one of the best-known American authors.

1. According to the character sketch above, Poe wrote all of the following except:
   A. "The Fall of the House of Usher"
   B. "The Valley of Unrest"
   C. "For Alice"
   D. "The Raven"

2. Poe's most popular tales are filled with an atmosphere of:
   A. the popular, the strange, and the terrible
   B. the strange, the bizarre, and the terrible
   C. love, beauty, and aspiration
   D. innocence, wonder, and beauty

3. Poe's best-known poem and one of the most famous works in American literature is:
   A. "To Helen"
   B. "Annabel Lee"
   C. "For Annie"
   D. "The Raven"

Total Problems:	Total Correct:	Score:

Name _____

Read the recipe and answer the questions that follow. Circle the letter beside the correct answer.

Making Pizza

Dough Ingredients
4 cups sifted all-purpose flour
1 package dry yeast
1 cup warm (85°) water
2 tablespoons vegetable or olive oil
1 teaspoon salt

Topping Ingredients
shredded mozzerella cheese
tomato sauce
pepperoni
Italian sausage
ham
sautéed onions
black olives
anchovies
chopped mushrooms
oregano

Directions
To make pizza dough, mix the ingredients as you would to make bread. Knead the dough for about 10 minutes. Cover with a damp cloth and let rise for about 2 hours. Oil two 14-inch pizza pans. Sprinkle a little flour over them. Pat and stretch the dough in the pans, pinching up a rim around the edges to hold the filling. Prick dough in about 6 places. Preheat the oven to 400°. Brush each pizza lightly with olive oil to prevent crust from becoming soggy. Spread the pizza with your favorite cheese and tomato sauce. Add toppings as desired. Let the pizza sit for 10 minutes. Bake about 25 minutes or until light brown. Serve at once.

1. When making pizza, what is the second thing that you do?
   A. Sprinkle a little flour over all.
   B. Knead the dough for about 10 minutes.
   C. Cover with a damp cloth.
   D. Let the dough rise for about 2 hours.

2. All but one of the following items is a suggested topping:
   A. black olives
   B. mushrooms
   C. pepperoni
   D. hamburger

3. How many minutes does it take to bake the pizza?
   A. 10 minutes
   B. 25 minutes
   C. 14 minutes
   D. 400 minutes

| Total Problems: | Total Correct: | Score: |

Name _____

Read the recipe and answer the questions that follow. Circle the letter beside the correct answer.

Preparing Vegetable Soup

Ingredients

2 tablespoons of bacon fat or butter
$\frac{1}{4}$ cup diced carrots
$\frac{1}{2}$ cup diced onions
$\frac{1}{2}$ cup diced celery
3 cups hot water or stock
1 cup canned tomatoes

$\frac{1}{2}$ cup pared, diced potatoes
1 tablespoon chopped parsley
$\frac{1}{2}$ teaspoon salt
$\frac{1}{4}$ teaspoon pepper
1 cup chopped cabbage

Directions

Place the bacon fat or butter in a large kettle. Sauté the carrots, onions, and celery, and add them to the kettle. Add the hot water or stock, tomatoes, potatoes, parsley, salt and pepper. Cover and cook about 35 minutes. Add the cabbage and cook about 5 minutes more. Remove from heat and let stand at least 5 minutes before serving. Makes about 6 cups.

---

1. What is the first thing to do in preparing the vegetable soup?
   A. Cut and dice the potatoes.
   B. Chop 1 cup of cabbage.
   C. Add 3 cups of hot water.
   D. Place 2 tablespoons of fat or butter in a kettle.

2. After the fat or butter, what ingredients are added next?
   A. onions, potatoes, and tomatoes
   B. carrots, onions, and celery
   C. tomatoes, potatoes, and parsley
   D. salt and pepper

3. After all the ingredients have been added to the kettle, how much longer do you cook the vegetable soup?
   A. 30 minutes
   B. 35 minutes
   C. 5 minutes
   D. 6 minutes

4. What do you do after you have sautéed the carrots, onions, and celery?
   A. Add 1 tablespoon of chopped parsley.
   B. Add 3 cups of hot water or stock.
   C. Cook about 5 minutes.
   D. Sauté briefly in the fat or butter.

Total Problems: _____ Total Correct: _____ Score: _____

Read the laboratory investigation and answer the questions that follow. Circle the letter beside the correct answer.

Measuring Your Pulse Rate

Problem: What are the effects of activity on pulse rate?
Materials: (per group) clock or watch with second hand; graph paper

Procedure:
1. On a separate sheet of paper, construct a data table similar to the one below.
2. Place the index and middle fingers from one hand on the opposite wrist where your wrist joins the base of your thumb. Move the two fingers slightly until you locate your pulse.
3. To determine your pulse rate, have a classmate or family member observe a clock or watch with a second hand as you count the number of beats that you feel in 60 seconds. Record the result.
4. Walk in place for one minute. Measure your pulse and record the result.
5. Run in place for one minute. Again, measure your pulse and record the result.
6. Sit down and rest. Measure your pulse after you have been resting for one minute and again after three minutes. Enter these results in your data table.
7. Use the data table to construct a bar graph, comparing each activity and the pulse rate you measured.

Observations:
1. What was the pulse rate you recorded in step 3? This is called your pulse rate at rest. How does your rate compare with those of your family or friends? (Do not be alarmed if your pulse rate is somewhat different from others.)
2. What effect did walking have on your pulse rate?
3. What effect did resting after running have on your pulse rate?

Activity	Resting	Walking	Running	Resting (1 minute after exercise)	Resting (3 minutes after exercise)
Pulse Rate					

1. According to step 6, which of the following is not directed?
   A. Measure your pulse after resting for three minutes.
   B. Measure your pulse after resting for one minute.
   C. Indicate your data in the table.
   D. Stand still to rest.

2. Which of the following materials is necessary for the investigation?
   A. globe
   B. clock
   C. ruler
   D. running trail

Read the passages and answer the questions that follow. Circle the letter beside the correct answer.

Music Therapy

Music therapy is a growing field that uses music to help patients recover or cope with life experiences. It is an established health profession in which music is used within a therapeutic relationship to address physical, emotional, cognitive, and social needs of individuals. Practiced all over the world, music therapy is becoming a very important medical field in today's society. Hospital intensive care units, nurseries, and operating rooms across the country are playing music for patients. From Alzheimer's disease with the elderly, to neurological disorders with children, music therapy can affect everyone. Of the elements in music—melody, harmony, rhythm, and intensity—it is rhythm that is the leading therapeutic factor. Everyday, people use music to help them cope with stress and to relax. Now, the medical profession is using this centuries' old art as a therapeutic tool.

1. Which one of the following statements is false?
   A. Music therapy is used to address emotional and social needs of individuals.
   B. Music therapy has only been around for about three hundred years.
   C. In music therapy, rhythm is the leading therapeutic factor.
   D. Practiced all over the world, music therapy is becoming a very important medical field in today's society.

The Holocaust

The Holocaust represents the ruthless massacre of eleven million people during World War II. Six million Jews, approximately two-thirds of Europe's total Jewish population, were brutally murdered by the Nazi regime between the years of 1933-1945. However, the Jewish people were not the only innocent civilians affected by this cruel act. Gypsies, Slavs, and homosexuals were also included in the genocide.

Adolf Hitler was a driving force in the Nazi movement. His rise to power thrust the world into the worst war in history. Hitler set out to recreate the world. His goal was to build an everlasting empire. He believed that his mission could not be complete without the extermination of Jewish men, women, and children.

2. Which one of the following statements is true?
   A. The Holocaust, under the direction of the Nazi Regime, occurred in 1945-1953.
   B. Hitler believed his mission could not be complete without the elimination of Asians.
   C. Gypsies, Slavs, and homosexuals were also persecuted by Hitler.
   D. The Holocaust represents the massacre of eleven thousand individuals.

| Total Problems: | Total Correct: | Score: |

Read each passage and answer the question that follows. Circle the letter beside the correct answer.

Cloning

Today's method for cloning animals is slightly different than the method used by Robert Briggs and Thomas King in the 1950s. The method most commonly used today is often referred to as the "Dolly the Sheep" method. In the Dolly method, a donor nucleus is joined with an egg cell that no longer has a nucleus. In this method, the scientists first obtain epithelial cells from the mammary glands and grow them in a culture dish. Next, the cells are gradually starved. The lack of nutrients causes the cells to go into a hibernation-like state in which the cells stop growing and multiplying. Then, the nuclei are removed from immature egg cells. The scientists extract the nuclei from the mammary cells and inject them into the enucleated eggs. The eggs are then given an electric jolt, which tricks the eggs into acting like fertilized eggs and causing them to divide. An egg is then placed into the uterus of the female animal that donated the eggs. At the end of the gestation period, a clone of the animal that donated the mammary cells is born.

1. What is another word that means the same as "clone?"
   A. friend
   B. difference
   C. look-alike
   D. enemy

Angels

Angels are an increasingly popular topic for movies and television shows. On one television series, two angels are the main characters. By tuning in to any Top 40 radio station, a listener can hear any number of songs mentioning angels. The diffusion of angels into pop culture has changed the public's opinion of angels. In a 1988 Gallup poll, fifty percent of adult Americans said they believed in angels. However, in a recent *TIME* magazine poll, almost seventy percent believed in angels, and only twenty-five percent said they did not believe in angels. Obviously, more people believe in angels now than just a decade ago.

2. According to this passage, what has accounted for the increase in the number of people who believe in angels?
   A. More newspapers now have "Angel" columns.
   B. More television shows, movies, and songs are about angels.
   C. There are more ministers preaching about angels.
   D. More and more people are watching television.

Read each passage and answer the question that follows. Circle the letter beside the correct answer.

Civil Engineering

There are many buildings constructed and designed by ancient engineers. The Great Pyramid and the Coliseum of Rome are just two examples of very well known buildings created by civil engineers. The Great Pyramid, which is 481 feet tall, was constructed in Egypt around 3,000 B.C. The pyramid consists of 2.25 million stone blocks averaging 1.5 tons a piece. The ancient Egyptians developed very complex archtectural techniques. Countless men spent years working tirelessly to erect the Great Pyramid and other classic buildings such as the Coliseum in Rome (built in 80 A.D.) Our word "architect" comes from "Architkton"—a Greek word for the person who was in charge of all the craftsmen, masons, and carpenters.

1. Which one of the following statements is false?
    A. The Great Pyramid in Greece has over 2 million stone blocks.
    B. Each stone block of the Great Pyramid averages 1.5 tons.
    C. The Coliseum in Rome was built around 80 A.D.
    D. The architkton was in charge of all the carpenters.

The Stock Exchange

There are many stock exchanges all over the world where stocks or shares of business are bought and sold. There are fourteen stock exchanges in the United States alone, and nine in Japan. The New York Stock Exchange is the largest exchange in the United States. Today, it is run by a board of twenty members and a member-elect chairman, but has 1,366 members who trade in securities. Trades can only be made by these members. To become a member, a "seat" can be purchased, inherited, or given as a gift. The "seats" then become personal property. The cost of a seat can be as much as $320,000.

2. Which one of the following statements is true?
    A. Japan has fourteen stock exchanges in its country.
    B. There are 1,866 members of the New York Stock Exchange.
    C. The United States has nine stock exchanges.
    D. New York has the largest stock exchange in the United States.

Total Problems:	Total Correct:	Score:

Read each passage and answer the question that follows. Circle the letter beside the correct answer.

Wildlife Conservation

Convinced of the enormous destructive power of human kind, pioneer conservationists of the early twentieth century emphasized the ethical responsibility of their own generation to conserve resources. During the past 2,000 years, the world has lost, through extinction, well over 100 species or sub-species of mammals. Approximately two-thirds of these losses have occurred since the mid-nineteenth century. Many other species are threatened in addition to those mammals that are already extinct. The primary factor in the depletion of the world's fauna has been modern human society, either directly through excessive hunting, or indirectly through destroying natural habitats.

1. Which one of the following is not a factor in the depletion of the fauna?
    A. destroying natural habitats
    B. modern human society
    C. not enough planting in the spring
    D. excessive hunting

History of Basketball

Basketball acquired its biggest boost when it was included in the 1936 Olympic Games in Berlin. Basketball had finally arrived as a major sport. From then on, scholastic, collegiate, and professional basketball grew quickly. Many organizations were created, such as the American Basketball League, The National Basketball League, and the National Basketball Association (NBA). In 1967, a professional league called the American Basketball Association was formed. It merged with the NBA in 1976, forming a twenty-two team league. During the 1970s and 1980s, college basketball greatly increased in popularity. The NCAA Division I men's championship tournament now ranks among the major sport events of the year.

2. What event caused basketball to grow and become a major sport?
    A. 1936 Olympic Games in Munich
    B. a merger with the NCAA in 1976
    C. 1936 Olympic Games in Berlin
    D. an organization created to boost basketball

Total Problems:	Total Correct:	Score:

Read the passage and answer the questions on the following page.

Morocco

Morocco, located along the Atlantic coast of Africa, measures 565 miles (910 km) from north to south and 730 miles (1,170 km) from east to west. It has 1,140 miles (1,835 km) of coastline along the North Atlantic Ocean and the Mediterranean Sea. Morocco has three main land regions: the Coastal Lowlands, the Atlas Mountain Chain, and the Sahara. Fertile plains are located in the Coastal Lowlands. The Atlas Mountain Chain crosses the middle of Morocco from southwest to northeast. East and south of the mountains lies the barren, sunbaked Sahara.

In Morocco, Arabs constitute the majority of the population, although Berbers, the original inhabitants, constitute about one-third of the people. The Berbers, who form a larger minority in Morocco than in any other North African country, are concentrated in the mountains. Arabic is the official language, but various Berber dialects continue to be spoken. French is still widely used, especially in government and business. Islam is the official religion, to which almost 99% of the inhabitants adhere. About 30,000 Jews live in Morocco, and almost all of the Europeans there are Roman Catholic.

Perhaps the most important element in Moroccan social life is the extended family. Ordinarily the household includes two parents, unmarried children, and married sons with their families. When the father dies, married sons establish their own households. Sometimes in the crowded urban areas, sons leave home before their father dies. Many of the homes consist of one large room that serves as the kitchen, living room, sleeping quarters, and barn. In the desert areas, some Moroccans are quite nomadic and live in tents. Urban dwellers often live in small attached houses. The wealthy, however, live in modern apartment buildings or spacious homes while the poor live in sprawling slums called "bidonvilles" (tin can towns) on the outskirts of large cities.

About half of Morocco's labor force is engaged in agriculture. Large, mechanized farms cover about one-third of the land presently available for cultivation and account for 85% of the total agricultural output. Wheat and barley, sugar beets, rice, and cotton constitute the chief crops for domestic consumption. Citrus fruits, winter vegetables, and grapes for wine are the principal export crops.

Popular Moroccan dishes include lemon chicken, tajine (a meat stew with vegetables), and a pastry made with honey and almonds. Mint tea is the national drink. Moroccans eat with their fingers from a large communal dish.

Moroccans wear traditional clothing although city dwellers often combine traditional garments with western-style clothing. Men wear a jellaba, a loose-fitting hooded robe with long, full sleeves. Rural men wear a burnoose, a heavier garment. Men usually wear a turban or brimless cap. Women also wear a jellaba as an outer garment. Some Islamic women still cover their face with a veil.

Elementary and secondary school is free in Morocco. For children ages seven to thirteen, school is compulsory; however, less than 70% attend. Approximately 50% of adult Moroccans are literate.

The most popular spectator sports in Morocco are soccer and basketball. Gathering at cafes as well as visiting with family are important leisure activities.

Read each question. Circle the letter beside the correct answer.

1. All of the following statements are true except:
    A. Arabic is the official language of Morocco.
    B. The poor live in duplex apartments near the wealthy class.
    C. About half of Morocco's labor force is engaged in agriculture.
    D. Elementary and secondary school is free in Morocco.

2. The most important element in Moroccan social life is the:
    A. extended family
    B. traditional clothing
    C. communal dish
    D. language

3. School is mandatory for children ages:
    A. six to thirteen
    B. five to fifteen
    C. seven to sixteen
    D. seven to thirteen

4. The chief Moroccan crops for domestic consumption are all of the following except:
    A. wheat and barley
    B. sugar beets
    C. corn
    D. cotton

5. The poor live in sprawling slums called:
    A. tajine
    B. burnoose
    C. jellaba
    D. bidonvilles

| Total Problems: | Total Correct: | Score: |

Read the poem and answer the questions on the following page.

Camouflaged

My parents don't understand me,
but they try to.

I see the trees,
but only hear the birds.

My sister says she cares,
but I can't tell.

My teachers think I am smart,
but I only do what they say.

My peers think they know me,
but do I know them?

My boyfriend and I sometimes do homework together,
but we never have real conversations.

My English class expects me to give the right answers,
but I need answers of my own.

I want to do something great,
but what's holding me back?

Sometimes I wonder who I really am.
I wonder.

Read each question. Circle the letter beside the correct answer.

1. The word "camouflage" means:
   A. confusing
   B. open
   C. hidden
   D. provoking

2. Possibly, the main idea of this poem is:
   A. friends don't understand the speaker
   B. conflicts within the self and relationships with others
   C. wanting to do something which seems impossible
   D. feeling egotistical and self-centered

3. Possibly, another word for the word "peers" in line 9 is:
   A. siblings
   B. enemies
   C. relatives
   D. classmates

4. Which two types of imagery are presented in lines 3 and 4?
   A. sight and sound
   B. smell and feeling
   C. sight and feeling
   D. sight and smelling

5. "Sometimes I wonder who I really am," in line 17, suggests that the speaker:
   A. thinks she is adopted
   B. thinks she is doing some bad things
   C. is involved in self-reflection
   D. has had an episode of amnesia

Read the poem and answer the questions on the following page.

Billy Bowman

One Saturday Billy Bowman was on his way
to get his fine horse some hay.
He stopped at Mrs. Bea's
for biscuits and tea.
Then he continued on his way.

Billy Bowman kept on his way
to get his fine horse some hay.
He stopped at Cindy Lou's
to watch the noontime news.
Then he continued on his way.

Billy Bowman traveled on his way
to get his fine horse some hay.
He stopped at the the Hound and the Deer
for his favorite game of billiards.
Then he continued on his way.

Billy Bowman continued on his way
to get his fine horse some hay.
He left in the morning,
traveling here and traveling there.
Then he continued on his way.

Billy Bowman bought the hay
and knew he must be on his way.
For his fine horse was a beautiful bay
out in the pasture where he lay.
Returning before sundown in the calm of the day.

Read each question. Circle the letter beside the correct answer.

1. "He stopped at The Hound and Deer for his favorite game of billiards." What are the context clues that indicate what The Hound and the Deer is?
   A. "He stopped" suggests office
   B. "game of" suggests gym
   C. "billiards" suggests club
   D. "for his favorite" suggests store

2. For what purpose was Billy Bowman traveling?
   A. to see Cindy Lou
   B. to get hay for his horse
   C. to sell some of his hay
   D. to see the countryside

3. What is noticeable about lines 1, 2, and 5 in all the stanzas?
   A. pun
   B. personification
   C. simile
   D. rhyme

4. A lesson that Billy Bowman teaches concerning pets and animals is:
   A. Don't shun and ignore responsibilities.
   B. Don't have a horse as a responsibility.
   C. Don't buy biscuits from Mrs. Bea.
   D. Don't play billiards in the Hound and the Deer.

5. Why did Billy Bowman stop at Cindy Lou's?
   A. to ask her hand in marriage
   B. to watch the noontime news
   C. to get hay for his horse
   D. to play his favorite game of billiards

6. When Billy Bowman left that morning, he was "traveling here and traveling there." This line probably suggests that:
   A. He had many errands to attend to that day.
   B. He didn't know where he was going.
   C. He became lost and had a difficult time getting back home.
   D. He bought hay from several different people.

Total Problems: Total Correct: Score:

Read the poem and answer the questions that follow. Circle the letter beside the correct answer.

Nature Is

Nature is a polar bear
running alongside her cub.
Nature is a mockingbird
singing a beautiful song.
Nature is a salmon
finding its way in the stream.

Nature is the rain
watering the earth.
Nature is the stars, the moon,
the pendulum of the seasons.
Nature is a voice.
See and know me, it cries.

Nature is beauty.
Nature is creation.

1. What is one noticeable difference between the first stanza and the second stanza?
   A. The first is about animal life, and the second is about the physical earth and universe.
   B. The first is about a fish, and the second is about a mockingbird.
   C. The first is about beauty, and the second is about creation.
   D. The first is about winds, and the second is about animals.

2. In line 10, the seasons are compared to a pendulum. This is called:
   A. metaphor
   B. alliteration
   B. simile
   D. paradox

3. The main idea of the poem is:
   A. Nature is a beautiful creation.
   B. the positive forces in nature
   C. the negative forces in nature
   D. Nature cannot be trusted anytime.

Name _____

Read the poem and answer the questions that follow. Circle the letter beside the correct answer.

The Land of Dreams

Under the sky
where the dragons fly
is a land by the sea.

A land of kings
where the Sirens sing,
a place where myths can be.

Creatures of old
fight the men who are bold
in epic battles of might.

Courage and fear
joy and tears,
where the losers run in fright.

Legends come alive
in a land that seems to thrive
only in our dreams.

1. Where is the land found that the narrator mentioned many times in the poem?
   A. mythology   B. battles   C. sea   D. dreams

2. In line 5, the word "Sirens" is a reference in Greek mythology to the women who lived on an island and lured sailors to the island and immediate death. This reference is a literary writing technique called:
   A. simile   B. metaphor   C. allusion   D. pun

3. In lines 7 and 8, the two words "old" and "bold" are examples of:
   A. end rhyme   B. rhythm   C. internal rhyme   D. beat

4. In line 5, the words "Sirens sing" represent an example of:
   A. personification B. alliteration   C. paradox   D. consonance

5. The word "myth" suggests that the information given is:
   A. from Greece   B. factual   C. fiction   D. historical

6. In line 9, another word for "might" is:
   A. strength   B. weakness   C. possibility   D. uneven

Total Problems: _____   Total Correct: _____   Score: _____

Read the poem and answer the questions on page 64.

Lyle the Frog

One pretty summer day,
Darren arrived in quite dismay
to a quaint little hole
of Harry the mole.
Harry welcomed the butterfly
who had a friend at his side.
The friend's name was Lyle,
the most well-known frog for miles.
Darren was perplexed with his nerves in a ball.
There was a problem he saw.
Harry asked Darren what was wrong,
and why exactly was his face so long?
Darren cried "TV," and Harry didn't understand.
Harry had thought TV was the greatest thing on land.
Finally, Darren introduced Lyle to Harry.
To Harry, Lyle didn't look so scary.
"How do you do?" to Lyle, asked Harry.
But "Remote" is how Lyle replied, somewhat wary.
Harry just stood there not knowing;
if he thought it was funny, he sure wasn't showing
why this response was not right.
Or maybe Lyle just isn't bright.
Once again, Harry asked, "How are you?"
Once again, Lyle said "Remote," as if he had no clue.
Darren began making a scene,
jumping and screaming, "See what I mean?
TV's done this to Lyle!
It's the worse case I've seen in a while.
He sits there and watches it all day;
he needs help in the worst of ways!"
Harry said he'd help but didn't know how,
and he could tell Darren didn't either by his raised eyebrow.
They sat there and thought of what to do

and realized just like Lyle—everything seemed taboo.

They knew that Lyle had to stop

before his brain became skip and hop.

He had watched TV so much he repeated all he heard.

It was beginning to get a little absurd.

Darren and Harry began reading books to him

to make his vocabulary not quite so slim.

They played music in his ears.

They listened so much they broke into tears.

They tried so hard with all their might;

They started in morning, and then it was night.

They thought what if Lyle still replied, "Remote"

to everything he saw and heard?

But they had to give it a try anyway,

hoping "Remote" wasn't all he would ever say.

After weeks of effort, Darren said, "Lyle, what's going on?"

Harry and Darren saw something that suggested they had won.

Lyle looked as if he understood what Darren had said,

then he began to raise his head.

"Not much," replied Lyle ever so slowly.

"Hooray!" shouted Harry as he jumped for glee.

"It worked! It worked!" yelled Darren with a smile.

"I'm cured! I have control again!" exclaimed Lyle.

"I've watched way too much TV for a person my age;

I could have been playing or acting on stage!

But now it is all over and I am so glad,

I've learned that too much TV is bad."

Lyle was thankful he had such good friends,

and he knew on them he could always depend.

Lyle went home that day and didn't turn on the telly;

instead, he read an interesting book about a frog's belly.

He would never be that hooked again, he thought,

and think he was somewhere in which he was naught.

Read each question. Circle the letter beside the correct answer.

1. The main idea of this poem is:
    A.   Frogs are smarter than most people think.
    B.   Too much television is bad.
    C.   It is good to have a butterfly for a friend.
    D.   Words are sometimes confusing and annoying.

2. In the story, Darren is the:
    A.   mole
    B.   chipmunk
    C.   frog
    D.   butterfly

3. How do Darren and Harry help Lyle to overcome his one-word vocabulary?
    A.   They enroll him in a private school near the pond.
    B.   They teach him phonics, one word at a time.
    C.   They read books and played music for Lyle.
    D.   They hire a tutor who instructs him every day.

4. After Lyle was cured and went home that day, the first thing he did was:
    A.   read a book about a frog's belly.
    B.   go home and turn on the telly.
    C.   hop to the pond and meet some old friends.
    D.   buy an airline ticket to London to celebrate his cure.

5. ". . . and think he was somewhere in which he was naught." In this line of the poem, naught means:
    A.   brilliant
    B.   light
    C.   decent
    D.   nothing

6. The only word spoken by Lyle before he was cured was:
    A.   Harry
    B.   Darren
    C.   Remote
    D.   Lyle

Total Problems:	Total Correct:	Score:

Name _____

Read the poem and answer the questions that follow. Circle the letter beside the correct answer.

Picture Day

Picture day!
What a fun treat.
There for a five-minute deal,
and always, a thirty-five minute ordeal.

On a stool with five little ones wiggling around.
Boys in the back, pushing and jumping.
Younger girl ripping a display present
and wanting her mother.

Two older grandchildren sitting looking bored,
waiting for at least one shot.
Photographer trying to get the youngsters' attention,
and doesn't seem to get anywhere.

Standing, waiting, and wondering—
why we are here?
Grandmother, everyone knows, patiently smiling
and waiting for the picture beside her bed.

1. Everyone is having a picture taken because:
    A. They don't have one.
    B. The two older grandchildren wanted to.
    C. The grandmother wanted a photograph of her grandchildren.
    D. The grandmother was a photographer.

2. What are the two older grandchildren doing?
    A. shopping for new jeans
    B. looking bored
    C. making funny faces at everyone
    D. helping the photographer

3. Another word for ordeal is:
    A. to play cards
    B. temperament
    C. trial or test
    D. wait

Total Problems:	Total Correct:	Score:

Read the poem and each question that follows. Circle the letter beside the correct answer.

Spring Song

Oh, what a glorious feeling to
step into that world of spring!
Burdens and responsibilities are
lifted from shoulders that can hold no more
and spring assaults the senses.

Eyes delight in the blossoming cherry tree
whose boughs gently sway in the cool breeze.
Lying on my back, I look up at the blue sky
where clouds gather like dreams
having taken flight from my mind.

Smells of freshly mowed grass are the
sweetest perfume,
joined by the sweet smell of the first yellow
roses climbing the trellis.
New life is everywhere!

Sweet tastes of honeysuckle,
blooming in abundance throughout the quiet
wood linger until a tart blackberry,
picked off the bush,
causes me to gasp in pleasant surprise.

The dogwood's trunk supports my back,
and the breeze in my hair soothes my spirit.
A tickling sensation on my arm alerts me
to the ant whose home I have
disturbed with a careless sweep of my hand.

Everywhere, the buzz of the bees,
the whispering trees, all sing in sweet accord.
The birds sing along, happy in their wedded bliss.
And my heart sings, too, to be a
part of the earth's spring song.

As day ends, night falls, bringing its own chorus.
The silvery moon sends beams to greet me,
and a star falls that I might make a wish.
"Oh, can every day be like this, free of care?
It's spring and I am glad to be alive!

1. In line 5, "spring assaults the senses," the best synonym for assaults would be:
    A. hits
    B. storms
    C. invades
    D. jumps on

2. In the second stanza, what has "taken flight from my mind?"
    A. dreams
    B. sky
    C. clouds
    D. boughs

3. According to the sixth stanza, which of the following does not "sing in sweet accord"?
    A. bees
    B. birds
    C. trees
    D. wolves

4. What happened to the ant's home?
    A. crushed by the narrator's foot
    B. blown away by a big grasshopper
    C. carried away by a big grasshopper
    D. destroyed by the narrator's hand

Total Problems: _____   Total Correct: _____   Score: _____

Refer to the mileage chart to answer each question. Write the answers in the blanks provided.

If you are planning a trip by car, you may want to consult a mileage table like the one below. To read the mileage table: 1) locate one of the cities in the left-hand column; 2) then, go across that row to the column headed by the other city's name. The number shown is the distance in road miles between the two cities.

Road Mileage	Atlanta, GA	Boston, MA	Chicago, IL	Denver, CO	Hartford, CT	Miami, FL	Omaha, NE	Seattle, WA
Albany, NY	991	166	836	1824	108	1405	1284	2909
Boston, MA	1075	X	1015	2003	102	1486	1463	3088
Cleveland, OH	481	648	355	1343	578	1235	803	2428
El Paso, TX	1425	2403	1483	624	2303	1938	1016	1695
Jackson, MS	383	1426	749	1223	1326	908	926	2521
Miami, FL	661	1486	1377	2077	1386	X	1660	3334
Pittsburgh, PA	683	593	472	1460	493	1168	920	2545
Wichita, KS	974	1627	720	515	1527	1608	310	1913

1. How far is it from:

   El Paso to Denver? _____ miles

   Albany to Chicago? _____ miles

   Miami to Atlanta? _____ miles

   Cleveland to Omaha? _____ miles

2. Which city is closest to:

   Jackson? _____

   Pittsburgh? _____

   Albany? _____

   Wichita? _____

3. Which city is farthest from:

   Boston? _____

   Miami? _____

   El Paso? _____

   Cleveland? _____

4. Is the distance greater between Albany and Chicago or between Cleveland and Chicago? _____

   How much greater? _____ miles

5. How many miles would you travel by road from Boston to Omaha? _____ miles

Total Problems:	Total Correct:	Score:

Refer to the bar graph to answer each question. Circle the letter beside the correct answer.

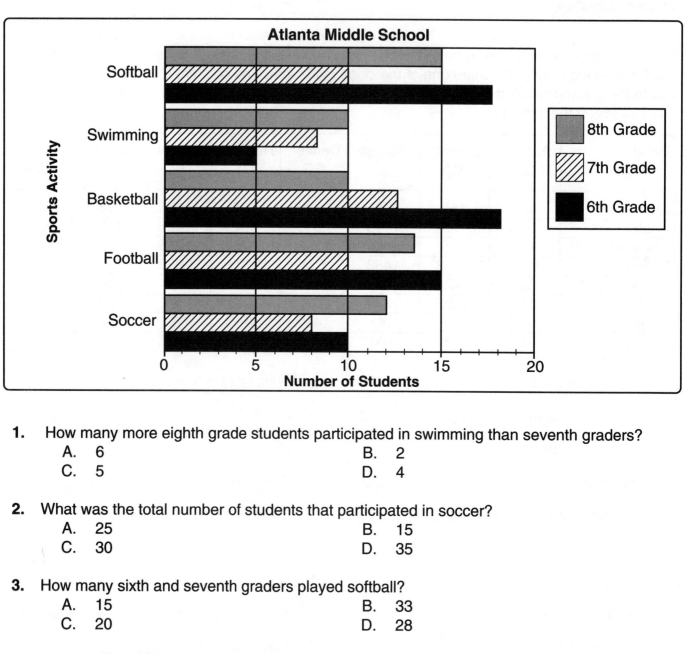

1. How many more eighth grade students participated in swimming than seventh graders?
   A. 6   B. 2
   C. 5   D. 4

2. What was the total number of students that participated in soccer?
   A. 25   B. 15
   C. 30   D. 35

3. How many sixth and seventh graders played softball?
   A. 15   B. 33
   C. 20   D. 28

4. What was the total number of seventh and eighth graders that played football?
   A. 23   B. 25
   C. 28   D. 32

5. How many more sixth grade students participated in basketball than seventh graders?
   A. 6   B. 10
   C. 8   D. 12

Total Problems:	Total Correct:	Score:

Name _____

Refer to the line graph to answer each question. Circle the letter beside the correct answer.

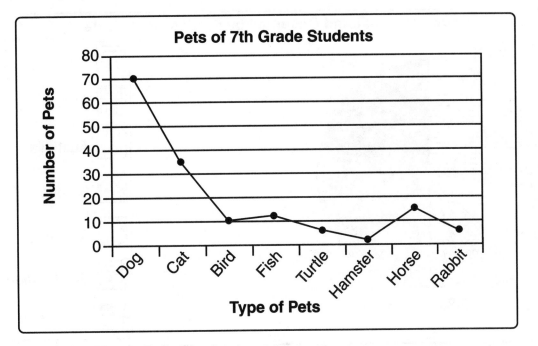

1. Of the seventh grade students polled, which pet was the least popular?
   A. turtle
   B. fish
   C. hamster
   D. rabbit

2. According to the poll, students had the same number of what two pets?
   A. turtles and hamsters
   B. fish and turtles
   C. hamsters and rabbits
   D. turtles and rabbits

3. How many more dogs than cats did the seventh graders own as pets?
   A. 30
   B. 35
   C. 20
   D. 40

4. How many horses did seventh grade students own as pets?
   A. 2
   B. 12
   C. 10
   D. 15

Total Problems:	Total Correct:	Score:

Refer to the pie graph to answer each question. Circle the letter beside the correct answer.

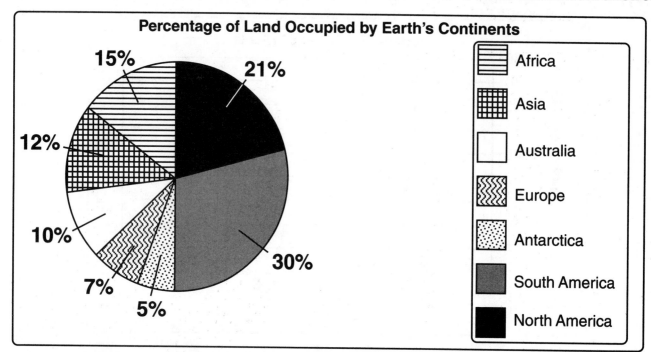

Percentage of Land Occupied by Earth's Continents

15%   21%

12%

10%

7%   5%   30%

Legend:
- Africa
- Asia
- Australia
- Europe
- Antarctica
- South America
- North America

1. Which continent covers the largest percentage of the earth's land surfaces?
   - A. Africa
   - B. Asia
   - C. North America
   - D. South America

2. Which continent covers the smallest percentage of the earth's land surfaces?
   - A. Australia
   - B. Europe
   - C. Antarctica
   - D. Africa

3. The pie graph represents what percent of the earth's land surface?
   - A. 85%
   - B. 90%
   - C. 95%
   - D. 100%

4. Which continent covers the second largest percentage of the earth's land surfaces?
   - A. Asia
   - B. North America
   - C. Africa
   - D. Australia

| Total Problems: | Total Correct: | Score: |

Refer to the map of northwestern Africa to answer each question. Circle the letter beside the correct answer.

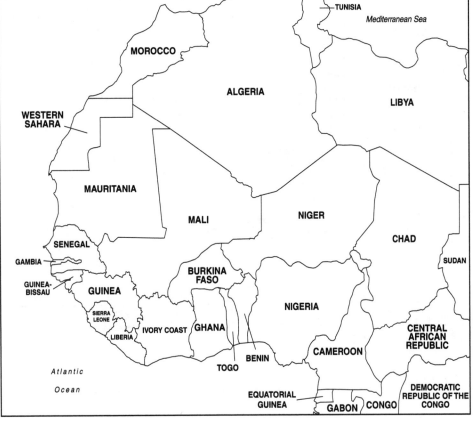

1. Libya is east of the country of:
    A. Niger   B. Algeria
    C. Mali   D. Tunisia

2. Togo is located between what two countries?
    A. Nigeria and Benin   B. Benin and Ivory Coast
    C. Ghana and Benin   D. Ghana and Nigeria

3. The largest country in northwest Africa is:
    A. Libya   B. Niger
    C. Mali   D. Algeria

4. Which country borders the northeast corner of Algeria?
    A. Mali   B. Morocco
    C. Tunisia   D. Libya

Total Problems: _____   Total Correct: _____   Score: _____

Refer to the map of Southeast Asia to answer each question. Circle the letter beside the correct answer.

1. What nation in Southeast Asia has only land borders?
    A. Myanmar
    B. Thailand
    C. Laos
    D. Cambodia

2. All of the following Southeast Asian countries are partly or entirely island countries except:
    A. Indonesia   B. Thailand
    C. Malaysia   D. Philippines

3. What country in Southeast Asia forms the tip of a peninsula?
    A. India   B. Thailand
    C. Cambodia   D. Malaysia

4. All of the following bodies of water surround Southeast Asia except:
    A. Atlantic Ocean   B. Pacific Ocean
    C. Indian Ocean   D. South China Sea

Total Problems: _____   Total Correct: _____   Score: _____

Read each question. Circle the letter beside the correct answer.

1. Your science teacher suggested that your class plant a cantaloupe field in the spring. If he wants you to plant the cantaloupe seeds at the right time of the moon, then you would consult the:
   A. *Bartlett's Book of Quotations*
   B. *The World Almanac and Book of Facts*
   C. *National Geographic Atlas*
   D. *Reader's Guide to Periodical Literature*

2. In which section of the newspaper would you find "Help Wanted" ads?
   A. sports section
   B. classified section
   C. entertainment section
   D. front page

3. If you had to find a word that has the same meaning as "solemn," you would look in:
   A. an encyclopedia   B. a telephone directory
   C. a thesaurus   D. an atlas

4. Where in a book do you find title, author, and publisher information?
   A. index   B. title page
   C. glossary   D. table of contents

5. If your history teacher asked you to bring in recent information on the Vice President and one of his recent trips abroad, you would probably look in:
   A. an encyclopedia   B. a card catalog
   C. a dictionary   D. a newspaper

6. Your family is going to the island of Rhodes. You don't know where this island is located. To find out where this island is located in the world, you would probably look in:
   A. a biographical dictionary   B. a thesaurus
   C. an atlas   D. a card catalog

7. You are doing research on the Biltmore Estate near Asheville, North Carolina. If you wanted general information on this famous house, you could look in:
   A. an encyclopedia   B. *Reader's Guide to Periodical Literature*
   C. a thesaurus   D. *International Who's Who*

8. Your English teacher asked you to find the meaning of "rheumatic." You would look in:
   A. an atlas   B. a thesaurus
   C. a dictionary   D. an encyclopedia

Refer to the dictionary entry to answer the questions at the bottom of the page. Circle the letter beside the correct answer.

---

ride

ride (rīd) v. **rode** (rōd), **rid•den** (`ri-dən), **rid•ing,** **rides** -*intr.* 1. To be carried or move, as in a vehicle or on horseback; *ride in a car.* 2. To travel over a surface; *The car rides smoothly.* 3. To be carried along; move as if on water; *rode to victory on a wave of public support.* 4. To depend on; *My grade rides on the results of the test.* 5. To allow to continue; *Let the problem ride. -tr.* 1. To sit on and move or drive: *ride a bicycle; ride a horse.* 2. To travel over, along, or through; *a delivery van riding the back roads.* 3. To be supported on; *surfers riding the waves.* 4. To take part in by riding; *a jockey riding the fourth race.* 5. Informal. To tease or ridicule. -*n.* 1. The act or an instance of riding, as in a vehicle or on an animal. 2. A device, such as one at an amusement park, that one rides for pleasure or excitement. 3. A means of transportation; *waiting for her ride to come.*

---

1. Which numbered definition means "to allow to continue?"
   A. 2
   B. 3
   C. 4
   D. 5

2. What is the part of speech for the word ride which means "a means of transportation?"
   A. adjective
   B. noun
   C. adverb
   D. verb

3. In the sentence "The car rides smoothly," what part of speech is "rides?"
   A. adjective
   B. noun
   C. adverb
   D. verb

4. What is definition #3 for "ride" when it is used as a transitive verb?
   A. to be supported on
   B. to take part in by riding
   C. to sit on and move or drive
   D. to travel over, along, or through

Refer to the Reader's Guide to Literature entry and the sample Title Page to answer the questions that follow each. Circle the letter beside the correct answer.

> Grooming Your Golden Retriever [taking care of your dog]
> D. Livingston. il Pets in the Field v.98 no 10 p 38-42 Mr 9 99

1. What is the name of the article in the entry above?
   A. "Taking Care of Your Dog"
   B. D. Livingston
   C. "Grooming Your Golden Retriever"
   D. Pets in Field

2. Where is the article found, according to the entry above?
   A. Pets in the Field
   B. D. Livingston
   C. Taking Care of Your Dog
   D. Grooming Your Golden Retriever

3. In which month and year is the article found?
   A. May 1998
   B. May 1962
   C. March 1999
   D. March 1962

Title Page

> *All About Cats*
>
> James R. Harris
> Kimberly A. Payne
>
> Publications National, Inc.

4. Publications National, Inc., is the name of the
   A. author   B. publisher   C. book   D. city

5. Who wrote the book?
   A. James Randall Harris
   C. Kimberly Ann Payne
   B. Kimberly A. Payne and James R. Harris
   D. Ronald Harris and Frankie Payne

Refer to the computerized Card Catalog entry to answer each question. Circle the letter beside the correct answer.

Title: An Imposter in New York / by Michael Forsyth, with introduction by Jay Snowden
Author: Forsyth, Michael 1956
Published: Boston: White Press, c1993
Physical description: 220 p. : 24 cm
Notes: Lenny Noble, a newcomer to the Big Apple, becomes the talk of all the rich women until one late night a funny incident happens at a gala event and the true identity of Lenny is revealed.
Notes: Interest grade level: 7-9
Subject: Fiction
Subject: Humorous

1. According to the card catalog, what do we know about the book?
    A. The book is about a Bostonian newcomer called Lenny Noble.
    B. Lenny Noble dresses as a clown and juggles at a gala event.
    C. At a gala event, a group of rich women discover the true identity of Lenny.
    D. One late night a very serious situation occurred at a party to Lenny.

2. The person who wrote *An Imposter in New York* is:
    A. Jay Snowden
    B. White Press
    C. Michael Forsyth
    D. Lenny Noble

3. How many pages does the book contain?
    A. 1993
    B. 1956
    C. 24
    D. 220

4. For what grade level is this book intended?
    A. 2-4
    B. 5-8
    C. 7-9
    D. 9-12

5. What is the name of the publishing company?
    A. Forsyth Michael
    B. Jay Snowden
    C. White Press
    D. Big Apple

Total Problems: _____   Total Correct: _____   Score: _____

Refer to the table of contents below to answer the questions. Circle the letter beside the correct answer.

Table Of Contents

1. If your teacher asked you to create a travel brochure on the Blowing Rock, NC, you could probably find information on creating the travel brochure on what page?
    A. 16   B. 44   C. 64   D. 57

2. If you were seeking information on the origination of blue grass music, in which chapter would you most likely find the information?
    A. The Appalachian Mountains
    B. Chimney Rock, NC
    C. Appalachian Culture
    D. Appalachian People

3. From which entry would the following passage most likely come? "Most of the Appalachians have rocky soil. In valleys, where the soil is richer and more fertile, farmers grow tobacco."
    A. Tourist Attractions   B. Local Events
    C. Where to Stay   D. Geography of the Appalachians

Refer to the index to answer the questions at the bottom of the page. Circle the letter beside each correct answer.

INDEX

C
Cambodia 33, 44
Campaign for Nuclear Disarmament 50
Canada 5, 23
capitalism 15, 29, 56
Castro, Fidel 37, 39
Central America 36-37
Chernobyl 47, 53
Chiang Kai-shek 16
children's rights 51
Chile 36
China 16-17, 25, 39, 40-41, 47-50
Cultural Revolution 41, revolution 16
Churchill, Winston 27-29
Civil Rights Movement 50-51, 56
Clinton, William 43
Cold War 38-39, 52, 54, 56

Columbia 36
communication 5
Communism, See Soviet Union
computers 53
concentration camps 25, 27, 29
Cuba 37, 39, 47
Cultural Revolution 41
Czechoslovakia 22, 28, 39, 47
Czech Republic 47

D
Dalai Lama 40
D-Day 26
de Gaulle, Charles 26
democracy 19, 41, 44, 40-51, 55-56

1. If you wanted to find information on China's Cultural Revolution, on what page(s) would you look?
    A. 16-17   B. 47-50   C. 41   D. 25

2. If you were interested in learning more about capitalism, on what page(s) would you look?
    A. 15, 29, 56   B. 5, 23   C. 36-37   D. 47, 53

3. What page(s) would probably give you information about Winston Churchill?
    A. 40-41   B. 16   C. 50   D. 27-29

4. If you were writing a research paper on concentration camps, on what page(s) would you look?
    A. 23, 25, 27   B. 25, 27, 29   C. 37, 39, 47 D. 22, 28, 39

5. Which one of the following statements about the index is not true?
    A. Information on China can be found in at least 10 places.
    B. Each topic is followed by a page number where the information can be found.
    C. The index gives definitions of words and phrases.
    D. The topics are listed alphabetically.

Total Problems:	Total Correct:	Score:

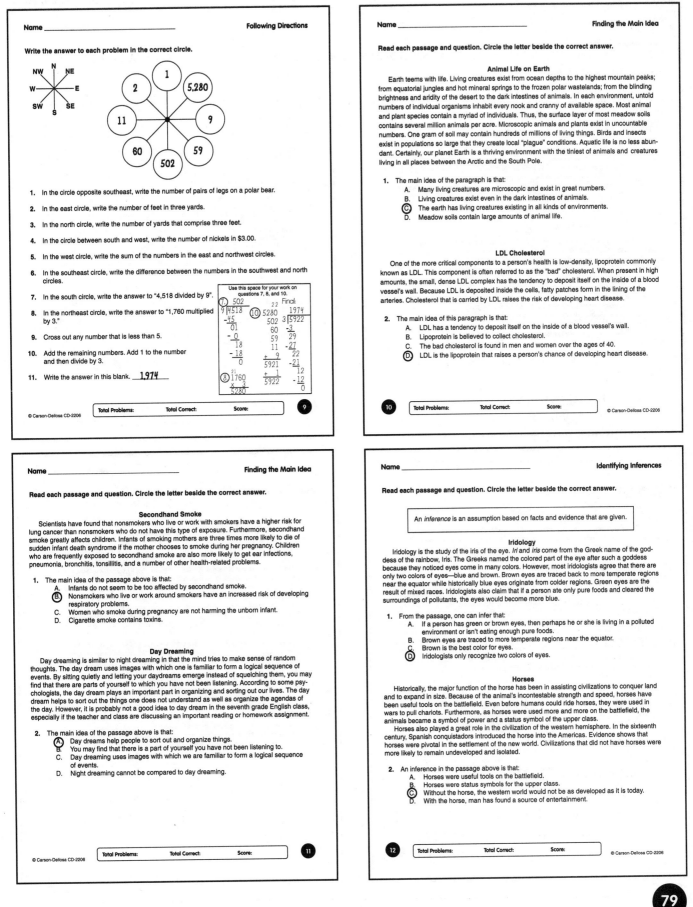

Following Directions

Name _____

Write the answer to each problem in the correct circle.

Circles: 1, 2, 5,280, 11, 9, 60, 59, 502

Compass: NW N NE / W E / SW S SE

1. In the circle opposite southeast, write the number of pairs of legs on a polar bear.

2. In the east circle, write the number of feet in three yards.

3. In the north circle, write the number of yards that comprise three feet.

4. In the circle between south and west, write the number of nickels in $3.00.

5. In the west circle, write the sum of the numbers in the east and northwest circles.

6. In the southeast circle, write the difference between the numbers in the southwest and north circles.

7. In the south circle, write the answer to "4,518 divided by 9".

8. In the northeast circle, write the answer to "1,760 multiplied by 3."

9. Cross out any number that is less than 5.

10. Add the remaining numbers. Add 1 to the number and then divide by 3.

11. Write the answer in this blank. __1,974__

Use this space for your work on questions 7, 8, and 10.

```
7) 502          22   Final:
 9)4518    10) 5280  1974
   -45         502  3)5922
    01          60   -3
   - 0          59   29
    18          11  -27
   -18         + 9   22
     0        5921  -21
    21        + 1    12
 8)1760       5922  -12
   x 3                0
   5280
```

Total Problems: _____ Total Correct: _____ Score: _____ 9

© Carson-Dellosa CD-2206

Finding the Main Idea

Name _____

Read each passage and question. Circle the letter beside the correct answer.

Animal Life on Earth

Earth teems with life. Living creatures exist from ocean depths to the highest mountain peaks; from equatorial jungles and hot mineral springs to the frozen polar wastelands; from the blinding brightness and aridity of the desert to the dark intestines of animals. In each environment, untold numbers of individual organisms inhabit every nook and cranny of available space. Most animal and plant species contain a myriad of individuals. Thus, the surface layer of most meadow soils contains several million animals per acre. Microscopic animals and plants exist in uncountable numbers. One gram of soil may contain hundreds of millions of living things. Birds and insects exist in populations so large that they create local "plague" conditions. Aquatic life is no less abundant. Certainly, our planet Earth is a thriving environment with the tiniest of animals and creatures living in all places between the Arctic and the South Pole.

1. The main idea of the paragraph is that:
   A. Many living creatures are microscopic and exist in great numbers.
   B. Living creatures exist even in the dark intestines of animals.
   C. The earth has living creatures existing in all kinds of environments.
   D. Meadow soils contain large amounts of animal life.

LDL Cholesterol

One of the more critical components to a person's health is low-density, lipoprotein commonly known as LDL. This component is often referred to as the "bad" cholesterol. When present in high amounts, the small, dense LDL complex has the tendency to deposit itself on the inside of a blood vessel's wall. Because LDL is deposited inside the cells, fatty patches form in the lining of the arteries. Cholesterol that is carried by LDL raises the risk of developing heart disease.

2. The main idea of this paragraph is that:
   A. LDL has a tendency to deposit itself on the inside of a blood vessel's wall.
   B. Lipoprotein is believed to collect cholesterol.
   C. The bad cholesterol is found in men and women over the ages of 40.
   D. LDL is the lipoprotein that raises a person's chance of developing heart disease.

10 Total Problems: _____ Total Correct: _____ Score: _____ © Carson-Dellosa CD-2206

Finding the Main Idea

Name _____

Read each passage and question. Circle the letter beside the correct answer.

Secondhand Smoke

Scientists have found that nonsmokers who live or work with smokers have a higher risk for lung cancer than nonsmokers who do not have this type of exposure. Furthermore, secondhand smoke greatly affects children. Infants of smoking mothers are three times more likely to die of sudden infant death syndrome if the mother chooses to smoke during her pregnancy. Children who are frequently exposed to secondhand smoke are also more likely to get ear infections, pneumonia, bronchitis, tonsillitis, and a number of other health-related problems.

1. The main idea of the passage above is that:
   A. Infants do not seem to be too affected by secondhand smoke.
   B. Nonsmokers who live or work around smokers have an increased risk of developing respiratory problems.
   C. Women who smoke during pregnancy are not harming the unborn infant.
   D. Cigarette smoke contains toxins.

Day Dreaming

Day dreaming is similar to night dreaming in that the mind tries to make sense of random thoughts. The day dream uses images with which one is familiar to form a logical sequence of events. By sitting quietly and letting your daydreams emerge instead of squelching them, you may find that there are parts of yourself to which you have not been listening. According to some psychologists, the day dream plays an important part in organizing and sorting out our lives. The day dream helps to sort out the things one does not understand as well as organize the agendas of the day. However, it is probably not a good idea to day dream in the seventh grade English class, especially if the teacher and class are discussing an important reading or homework assignment.

2. The main idea of the passage above is that:
   A. Day dreams help people to sort out and organize things.
   B. You may find that there is a part of yourself you have not been listening to.
   C. Day dreaming uses images with which we are familiar to form a logical sequence of events.
   D. Night dreaming cannot be compared to day dreaming.

Total Problems: _____ Total Correct: _____ Score: _____ 11

© Carson-Dellosa CD-2206

Identifying Inferences

Name _____

Read each passage and question. Circle the letter beside the correct answer.

An *inference* is an assumption based on facts and evidence that are given.

Iridology

Iridology is the study of the iris of the eye. *Iri* and *iris* come from the Greek name of the goddess of the rainbow, Iris. The Greeks named the colored part of the eye after such a goddess because they noticed eyes come in many colors. However, most iridologists agree that there are only two colors of eyes—blue and brown. Brown eyes are traced back to more temperate regions near the equator while historically blue eyes originate from colder regions. Green eyes are the result of mixed races. Iridologists also claim that if a person ate only pure foods and cleared the surroundings of pollutants, the eyes would become more blue.

1. From the passage, one can infer that:
   A. If a person has green or brown eyes, then perhaps he or she is living in a polluted environment or isn't eating enough pure foods.
   B. Brown eyes are traced to more temperate regions near the equator.
   C. Brown is the best color for eyes.
   D. Iridologists only recognize two colors of eyes.

Horses

Historically, the major function of the horse has been in assisting civilizations to conquer land and to expand in size. Because of the animal's incontestable strength and speed, horses have been useful tools on the battlefield. Even before humans could ride horses, they were used to pull chariots. Furthermore, as horses were used more and more on the battlefield, the animals became a symbol of power and a status symbol of the upper class.

Horses also played a great role in the civilization of the western hemisphere. In the sixteenth century, Spanish conquistadors introduced the horse into the Americas. Evidence shows that horses were pivotal in the settlement of the new world. Civilizations that did not have horses were more likely to remain undeveloped and isolated.

2. An inference in the passage above is that:
   A. Horses were useful tools on the battlefield.
   B. Horses were status symbols for the upper class.
   C. Without the horse, the western world would not be as developed as it is today.
   D. With the horse, man has found a source of entertainment.

12 Total Problems: _____ Total Correct: _____ Score: _____ © Carson-Dellosa CD-2206

© Carson-Dellosa CD-2206

Name _____   Identifying Inferences

Read each passage and question. Circle the letter beside the correct answer.

Patrick

Upon opening his door, a woman about twenty-five years old dashed past Patrick and into his living room.

"Help me! Please, sir!" she screamed, as she ran back to the door and locked it.

Patrick's mind went blank. Resorting back to his kindness—even in the midst of this horror—he sheltered her and began to speak boldly to her. "What are you doing? Who are you? Why are you in my apartment? What is going on?"

"I haven't the time, sir. Can I stay here for a short while?" she shouted.

Patrick shakily agreed.

1. An inference in the passage above is that:
   A. The girl has lost her way and needs time to think.
   B. The girl has lost the keys to her car and is trying to find them.
   C. The girl is being pursued by someone, and she needs a place to hide for a while.
   D. The girl's parents are looking for her, and their car is parked in front of his door.

Dreams

Dreamers who are female tend to dream of the two sexes equally and with equal encounters of hostility or friendliness. Unlike males, females normally dream of indoor or familiar settings; they often include conversations. Hostile dreams are more often verbally aggressive rather than physically aggressive. Females notice details, particularly of the other people in the dream. They notice facial features, colors, and other details.

2. An inference one can make from the above passage is that:
   A. Females normally dream of indoor or familiar settings.
   B. Males' dreams are often more verbally aggressive.
   C. Females and males often dream the same kinds of dreams.
   D. Males are more likely to dream of unfamiliar settings usually set outdoors.

Total Problems:	Total Correct:	Score:

© Carson-Dellosa CD-2206   **13**

Name _____   Arranging Sequence

Read the passage and answer the questions that follow. Circle the letter beside the correct answer.

Neil

At first Neil didn't realize where he was. Through blurry eyes and a tired little body, the room seemed strange and almost foreign, he thought. From what his senses could reveal, the furniture was stiff and seemed to have a new smell to it. Furthermore, he felt naked, wearing nothing but a long gown, which looked like something his grandmother would wear. As he eased up in the bed, still feeling drowsy, Neil realized where he was and what was going on. He still had the tube in his arm, but it didn't hurt. It was just annoying.

He was in a room by himself. He wasn't afraid, because he was eleven now and almost in middle school. Everyone had told him that his throat would feel this way, but soon he would begin to feel much better. Anyway, this was only the first full day since it happened.

Slightly propped-up on his pillow and still looking around, he saw the door open. She was smiling and wearing a funny-looking uniform with a white cap on her head. She asked him if he needed anything; maybe some ice cream, she suggested. Feeling quite sore, especially in the back of his mouth, Neil thought the ice cream might be soothing. Plus, he was a little hungry. He said he would take some pralines and cream—his favorite ice cream.

As the woman left his room, someone knocked on his door and said his name. He recognized the voices as those of his mom and dad. He tried to say "Come in," loudly, but his voice was weak and his throat was sore. His dad came over and gave him a little tug on the arm—not the one with the tube in it. He and his dad did all sorts of things together. They had planned to camp out this past weekend, but Neil had to come here instead.

Another knock on the door and the woman with the funny-looking cap came in with the ice cream. Boy, did it ever taste good! It felt good going down the back of his throat. His friend Brad had said that this was why they gave you ice cream at times like this. He said it was because you couldn't eat hard foods for a few days, and ice cream would be perfect. Neil thought he could eat ice cream like this for a week, and all he had to do was press the little button and someone would bring it to him.

1. Which event happened first?
   A. He tried to say "Come in," loudly, but his voice was weak and his throat was sore.
   B. Did it ever taste good; plus it felt good going down the back of his throat.
   C. As he eased up in his bed, still feeling drowsy, Neil realized where he was. . .
   D. She was smiling and wearing a funny-looking uniform with a white cap on her head.

2. One can draw what conclusion as to why Neil is in the hospital?
   A. He was playing soccer and had a serious facial injury.
   B. He is in the hospital to have his tonsils removed.
   C. He was in a car accident and was badly injured on the right side of his head.
   D. He was roller blading with Brad, and somehow Brad tripped him.

14 | Total Problems: | Total Correct: | Score: |
|---|---|---|

© Carson-Dellosa CD-2206

Name _____   Arranging Sequence

Read the passage and answer the questions that follow. Circle the letter beside the correct answer.

Brad Samson

Brad Samson was a music teacher who tried very hard to encourage his students. He had one student, Stephanie Adams, whom he thought had the potential to become a great singer. Stephanie had very little self-confidence, and when try-outs for the school musical were scheduled, she decided not to audition.

Brad approached Stephanie five days before the try-outs and asked her why she wasn't auditioning. Her only response was, "I'm just not good enough." Deep down inside, Brad knew that Stephanie wanted to audition, but just didn't have the courage to do it.

Stephanie was in the school choir and a few other school activities, but her real loves were singing and dancing. Every time Brad suggested that Stephanie audition, she would make excuses. One time she said she had to work, and the next time she said she had a major science project due. This continued for about three days, until finally Brad convinced her to try out.

The auditions went very well; many students participated, and Brad was impressed. Everyone was asked to sing, dance, and read selected monologues. The song Stephanie was asked to sing was one she knew, but she was still very nervous and unsure. The dance she performed was simple; she could have done this one with her eyes closed. After the judges turned in their points, Stephanie won by a great majority. She won the lead in the spring musical, just as Brad had predicted. Stephanie was on her way and Brad was very proud of her.

1. Which event happened first?
   A. The song Stephanie was asked to sing was one she knew.
   B. Deep down inside, Brad knew Stephanie wanted to audition.
   C. When musical try-outs were scheduled, Stephanie decided not to audition.
   D. This continued for about three days, until finally Brad convinced her.

2. Which one of the following events happened last?
   A. He had one student Stephanie Adams that he really thought had potential.
   B. After the judges turned in their points, Stephanie won by a great majority.
   C. One time she said she had to work, and the next she said that she had a science project due.
   D. Her only response was, "I'm just not good enough."

© Carson-Dellosa CD-2206 | Total Problems: | Total Correct: | Score: |
|---|---|---|
15

Name _____   Recognizing Supporting Details

Read the passage and answer the questions on the following page.

Timothy's Adventure

Timothy ran as fast as his little eight-year-old legs could take him. Running through the mud, he knew if he were to stop that it could get him. "What is it?" Timothy thought to himself. He felt he couldn't take one more step, or he would die from exhaustion. He looked to see if it was still there.

He turned and didn't see it, but as he turned to face the other way, he saw something out of the corner of his eye. It was the monster that he feared, a dog-like creature with beady red eyes and long, shaggy fur.

Quickly, he looked for cover, but the only place he could go was the cornfield that belonged to old man Harold Tutwiler. However, looking closer, he noticed on the other side of the cornfield was the remains of a dilapidated barn. He decided to make a run for it. Running as fast as he could through the field, Timothy heard the creature behind him. Almost panicking, he kept his pace, only expecting the worst in the end.

Reaching the barn and immediately trying to lock himself inside, he heard the monster clawing and making bone-chilling noises outside the barn door. He climbed into the barn loft and waited and listened. He sat there for hours, it seemed, but it was only for a few minutes.

"Thank God, I'm safe," Timothy said, in an unsure, quiet exclamation. He spoke too soon because at that moment the creature, panting heavily, broke through the door and glared at him. What was Timothy to do? The creature was blocking the only entrance in the barn; there were no windows or other doors. Stalking his prey with red hot eyes, the monster found Timothy hiding in the hay. In no time, the creature pounced on Timothy and bared his teeth. Timothy felt the creature's saliva dripping onto his face as the monster prepared to sink his teeth into Timothy's flesh.

Just at that moment Timothy awoke to find his dog Sparky, licking his face from one side to the other. Sweaty and relieved, Timothy realized it was only a dream.

16

© Carson-Dellosa CD-2206

Page 17 — Recognizing Supporting Details

Name _____   Recognizing Supporting Details

Read each question. Circle the letter beside the correct answer.

1. What does the creature look like?
   A. dog-like creature with beady, black eyes and long, shaggy fur
   B. dog-like bird with beady red eyes and long, shaggy fur
   C. dog-like creature with beady, red eyes and short, shaggy fur
   D. dog-like creature with beady, red eyes and long, shaggy fur *(D circled)*

2. Where does Timothy hide to escape the creature?
   A. a barn *(A circled)*
   B. a house
   C. a cornfield
   D. a school

3. In the third paragraph, what is another word that means the same as *dilapidated*?
   A. dingy red
   B. broken-down *(B circled)*
   C. renovated
   D. newly built

4. Who is Sparky?
   A. the name of the creature
   B. the name of the horse
   C. the name of Timothy's dog *(C circled)*
   D. the name of the bird

5. As the creature was about to bite Timothy, what did Timothy feel dripping onto his face?
   A. blood
   B. saliva *(B circled)*
   C. water
   D. corn

6. "Timothy's Adventure" is about a:
   A. real adventure a young boy had with a mean creature
   B. real adventure a young boy had while staying with his grandfather
   C. make-believe story that a young boy created to tell his friends
   D. bad dream that a young boy had *(D circled)*

Total Problems: _____ Total Correct: _____ Score: _____ **17**

© Carson-Dellosa CD-2206

Page 18 — Identifying Figurative Language

Name _____   Identifying Figurative Language

Figurative Language uses devices such as similes and metaphors to represent something else.
Examples: *The sky is cloudy and gray.* (Literal Language)
The sky is like a gray cat in the fog. (Figurative Language)

Read the poem and then circle the letter beside each correct answer.

Life

Watching and waiting to fulfill my dreams
I'm lying here wondering
where the road leads.
Years are behind me and still more ahead;
I don't want to waste another
moment here in this bed.
There is so much to do, so much to see,
and a big fence standing in front of me.
I want to leave, and I want to fly,
without taking the time
to even say good-bye.
I'm young and naive
in trust do you not believe?
Let me go; I want to live.
I have so much more to give.

1. In line 8, the word "fence" represents:
   A. a high wooden fence which the narrator cannot get over
   B. the prison to which the narrator has been sent
   C. an obstacle in the narrator's life *(C circled)*
   D. a detention home

2. The "road" in line 3, refers to the:
   A. interstate
   B. future *(B circled)*
   C. new four-lane road
   D. past

3. ". . . I want to fly" in line 9 is an example of a:
   A. metaphor *(A circled)*
   B. pun
   C. personification
   D. simile

4. There is a context clue that suggests that the speaker is actually "here in this bed," line 6. What is the clue?
   A. wondering
   B. watching
   C. dreams
   D. lying *(D circled)*

5. Another word for "naive" is:
   A. innocent *(A circled)*
   B. indifferent
   C. guilty
   D. restless

18 Total Problems: _____ Total Correct: _____ Score: _____

© Carson-Dellosa CD-2206

Page 19 — Identifying Figurative Language

Name _____   Identifying Figurative Language

Read the poem and circle the letter beside each correct answer.

Time Passes

A gust of wind blows,
and another leaf drops.
A baby is born,
and a husband goes off to work.

A young woman says, "I do,"
and a wife says, "Good bye."
Two friends embrace,
as they go their separate ways.

A boy wants to play soccer
and a girl wants to be an astronaut.
One grows up strong,
while the other grows up brave.

Dreams are fulfilled,
and others fade.
Promises are broken,
while commitments are made.

The sun begins to rise,
and a new day starts.
Time keeps passing,
while yesterday parts.

1. Lines 1 and 2 possibly suggest:
   A. a tornado
   B. life and death *(B circled)*
   C. a blight is killing the tree
   D. fall is on the way

2. "A baby is born" in line 3 employs the writing technique known as:
   A. simile
   B. metaphor
   C. paradox
   D. alliteration *(D circled)*

3. The words "fade" and "made," in lines 18 and 20 are examples of:
   A. rhythm
   B. internal rhyme
   C. end rhyme *(C circled)*
   D. alliteration

4. In the last two lines of the poem, "Time keeps passing, while yesterday parts," the meaning of the lines is:
   A. time passes, but yesterday divides into parts
   B. time passes, but yesterday is yet to come
   C. time passes, and yesterday goes away *(C circled)*
   D. time passes, but yesterday waits for tomorrow

5. The main idea of the poem is:
   A. dreams
   B. time *(B circled)*
   C. nature
   D. love

Total Problems: _____ Total Correct: _____ Score: _____ **19**

© Carson-Dellosa CD-2206

Page 20 — Finding Context Clues

Name _____   Finding Context Clues

Read the passage. As you consider the meanings of the italicized words, pay attention to the other words (clues) that surround the italicized words. Choose a word from the word bank that is closest in meaning to each italicized word. Write the correct word in the blank beside the italicized word. Not all words are used. Use a dictionary if necessary.

The Cricket

The lowly cricket is no ordinary insect. Although most insects are *loathed*, the cricket has many friends. For centuries, the Chinese and Japanese have kept crickets as pets in elaborate and *luxurious* cages. Friends of the cricket admire its *melodic* fiddling, the *gratifying* music of a relaxing summer evening. This admiration is not *unanimous*, however. Isaac Stern, a famous violinist, was once momentarily *vanquished* by a tiny competitor. He delayed a concert five minutes while attendants *feverishly* tried to find the tiny fiddler, who was happily *nestled* in a potted palm.

1. *loathed*   disliked
2. *luxurious*   costly
3. *melodic*   tuneful
4. *gratifying*   pleasant
5. *unanimous*   of one opinion
6. *vanquished*   defeated
7. *feverishly*   excitedly
8. *nestled*   settled

Word Bank			
careless	disliked	of one opinion	pleasant
costly	excitedly	opponents	tuneful
defeated	happily	settled	warlike

20 Total Problems: _____ Total Correct: _____ Score: _____

© Carson-Dellosa CD-2206

81

© Carson-Dellosa CD-2206

Name _____ Finding Context Clues

Read each sentence. As you consider the meanings of the italicized words, pay attention to the other words (clues) that surround the italicized words. Choose a definition to match each italicized word. Write the letter of the correct definition in the blank beside each sentence. Not all definitions are used.

1. __g__ An old tree in the front yard was his *haven* from the rest of society.

2. __d__ Although Jeremy is *fluent* in Spanish, he is very tongue-tied in German.

3. __j__ The lack of laws and leadership brought the country to a state of *anarchy*.

4. __f__ Be *wary* in situations such as walking alone on dark streets and swimming at night.

5. __i__ If Angie falls from the boat, throw her a life vest or another *buoyant* object.

6. __l__ All children can be protected from measles if they get a shot and become *immune*.

7. __h__ The *conspiracy* to assassinate President Lincoln was a plan that involved several people.

8. __a__ The lively conversation made up for the rather *mediocre* meal at the new restaurant.

9. __c__ Be sure to get a *competent* electrician, for one who is unskilled can't fix the wiring.

10. __b__ Josh was upset when the cab driver *meandered* around the park, for he had a plane to catch and didn't want to miss it.

Definitions
a. average
b. wandered aimlessly
c. qualified, skilled
d. able to speak effortlessly
e. sentimental
f. cautious
g. refuge or shelter
h. a secret agreement or plot
i. able to float
j. political disorder and confusion
k. good-natured
l. safe or unthreatened by

© Carson-Dellosa CD-2206 | Total Problems: ____ Total Correct: ____ Score: ____ | **21**

Name _____ Drawing Conclusions

Read the poem and the passage. Read the questions and circle the letter of the correct answer. Use context clues in order to draw conclusions about the passage.

What are little boys made of?
What are little boys made of?
Snakes and snails and puppy dog tails.
That's what little boys are made of.

What are little girls made of?
What are little girls made of?
Sugar and spice and everything nice.
That's what little girls are made of.

There are some fairy tales and rhymes that portray stereotypical sex or gender roles. Obviously, a child is born a certain sex, but he or she learns to adhere to a label and the pattern that society sets for him or her. Many of these learned influences will continue to exist; however, some of the problem is in literature and can be avoided. Gender stereotypes portray girls as angelic, and boys as rough and athletic.

1. After reading the rhyme above, what conclusion could you draw about boys?
   A. Little boys are made of snakes, snails, and puppy dog tails.
   B. Little boys like repetition.
   C. Little boys dislike sugar and spice.
   D. Little boys are likely to be interested in animals, such as snakes and dogs.

2. How is the rhyme above an example of gender stereotyping in literature?
   A. It says that boys will be boys, and girls will be girls.
   B. It implies that boys are closer to nature, while girls are domestic and refined.
   C. It says that all girls like sweets and candy.
   D. It implies that boys can get away with more than girls.

22 | Total Problems: ____ Total Correct: ____ Score: ____ | © Carson-Dellosa CD-2206

Name _____ New School and New Friends

Read the passage and answer the questions that follow.

New School and New Friends

When Olga and her family moved into Smithville, Olga was a little nervous. Making friends was not easy for her, and moving into a new town was not exactly how Olga had planned to spend her thirteenth birthday. But she had decided to make the best of the move and go to school the next day, instead of waiting until Monday. Her parents had told her that she could begin on Monday, but since it was only Wednesday and the weekend was close, she decided to go ahead and get the first day out of the way.

As the school day began, everyone was talking about the new Swedish girl that had just moved into town. Also, there was already a rumor going around that it was her birthday this weekend, and everyone wanted to be nice to her. The students in Smithville Middle School were unusually nice to people sometimes, and a large group of students decided to throw her a surprise birthday party at Jonathan Allen's lake house located just outside of town. Jonathan was an eighth grader, but everyone liked him. "I know this is hard on her," Laura Shipp said to Jonathan, "because it was really hard on me when I moved here three years ago." Laura remembered how she felt when she first moved here and wanted to make things easier for Olga.

Laura and her friends devised a plan: they would invite Olga to the lake with them this weekend, where everyone would surprise her with a birthday party.

"I'll find the biggest cake I can," Sherman Fincher said, "but it might be difficult to find one on such a short notice."

Laura added, "Don't worry too much about it. Olga is probably more interested in making friends than having a big cake. I know from my own experience." Chris agreed to bring lots of candy, and all the kids agreed to meet at Jonathan's lake house at 3 o'clock on Saturday afternoon.

Now the only thing left to do was to get Olga to come to the lake. Olga did seem to be a shy person to Laura and her friends, and they wondered if she would accept their invitation. As they approached her on Thursday afternoon, Olga would hardly take her eyes off the floor. "Hi, you're new here, aren't you?" Laura asked.

"Yeah," Olga answered sheepishly.

Laura wondered about their plan now, but she asked her anyway, "Well, we were talking and ... what's your name?"

"Olga," she answered, but continued to stare at the floor.

Laura quickly responded, "Well, Olga, we were talking and were wondering if you would like to come to the lake with us this weekend. It'll be fun."

© Carson-Dellosa CD-2206 | **23**

Name _____ New School and New Friends

Olga looked around to make sure that Laura was actually speaking to her directly. Finally, she said, "That sounds like fun."

Laura began to smile and said, "Great. I'll pick you up at 2:30 on Saturday afternoon."

When Laura and Olga arrived at the lake at 3 o'clock on Saturday, everyone was waiting and wearing their swimsuits. Olga didn't know how to swim, and she immediately felt a little uneasy. However, she decided to put that aside and try to have fun anyway. Everyone was swimming and playing in the water, but Olga didn't really want to get into the water just yet.

When they began to notice that Olga was not swimming with them, they got out of the water and gathered around her.

"Well, we knew that it was your birthday, and we have a big surprise for you. Happy Birthday. You do like cake, don't you?" asked Sherman.

"I do, but I'm diabetic. I don't think I can," said Olga, feeling sorry for her new friends.

Everyone just looked around at each other. They had tried so hard to make her feel welcome, but everything had turned out wrong. Finally, Laura spoke, "Olga, I'm sorry. We tried to have a nice party for you, but it seems that we have done everything wrong."

Olga just laughed and said, "That's all right. What I really wanted was some new friends at school, and that's what I have. Your friendship means more to me than the cake. Thank you so much."

After that afternoon, Olga and the gang became great friends. Olga's new friends learned an important lesson that day which helped them so much in and out of school.

24 | © Carson-Dellosa CD-2206

82

New School and New Friends

Name _____

Read each question. Circle the letter beside the correct answer.

1. What do you suppose is the important lesson that Olga's new friends learned that afternoon?
   A. Be careful when you are swimming in the lake.
   (B) Friendship is more important than gifts.
   C. Birthday parties are easy to plan for.
   D. Students from Sweden are more difficult to please than American students.

2. Where was the surprise birthday party held for Olga?
   A. Laura Shipp's house
   B. Sherman Fincher's house
   C. Laura's lake house
   (D) Jonathan Allen's lake house

3. Why can't Olga eat her birthday cake?
   A. She has been having some stomach problems lately.
   B. Her doctor insists that Olga is allergic to eggs and flour in cakes.
   C. She ate a big slice of chocolate cake before she attended the party.
   (D) She has diabetes and is not supposed to eat the cake.

4. "Olga didn't know how to swim, and she immediately felt a little apprehensive. However, she decided to put that aside and try to have fun anyway." What are the context clues for the meaning of the word "apprehensive"?
   (A) didn't know how to swim
   B. she decided to put that
   C. immediately felt
   D. try to have fun

5. Why didn't Olga want to swim in the lake?
   A. She forgot her swimsuit.
   B. Her parents wouldn't allow her to swim with other teenagers.
   (C) She didn't know how to swim.
   D. Because she was a diabetic, she wasn't supposed to get into the water.

Total Problems: _____ Total Correct: _____ Score: _____ **25**

26

Lucky Ike

Name _____

Read the passage and answer the questions on the following page.

Lucky Ike

Poor Ike. He didn't want much. He only wanted one thing in life—to play soccer. Ahh the money...the awards...the fame he'd have.

"Ike!" Coach Bull's bellowing voice snapped him back to his senses. "It's game time, Ike!"

"Oh yeah!" he replied.

He had forgotten for a moment. Today was the big game. Northwest Middle School was in the state soccer championship. If Ike was ever to shine, today was the day.

Ike sprinted out onto the field in front of the roaring crowd. He neared the middle of the field before he managed to get tangled in his shoelaces and fall flat on his face.

The crowd roared with laughter as Ike trotted toward his reserved spot on the bench. He squeezed in between the coach and the water cooler. He somehow hoped that the coach would notice him here and put him into the game.

By halftime, the game was a tie. During the second half, the broiling June heat had begun to affect both teams. Players became exhausted and then retired to the artificial coolness of the locker room. Soon, Ike found himself almost alone on the bench beside the coach.

"Oh no," sighed Coach Bull as another player collapsed.

"Wow!" thought Ike. "Now Coach has to play me because there is no one else."

"Well, I suppose you're our last hope, Ike," Coach Bull groaned.

Quickly Ike sprinted onto the field, this time keeping his balance. He wasn't in the game over three minutes before everything went into slow motion, just like a movie. The whistle screeched and the play resumed. The ball came to Ike, and he dove.

Pow! Lights flashed like some mad carnival.

Ike awoke to cheers in the hospital room. His team had won. Ike had hit his head on the goal post, and the goalie had laughed so hard that he didn't notice the ball scoot by into the goal.

"Well, I guess I did my part today," Ike said, as he rubbed his head where a goose egg was presently forming.

Lucky Ike

Name _____

Read each question. Circle the letter beside the correct answer.

1. One could say the story is mainly about:
   (A) a very awkward boy
   B. a mean coach
   C. avoiding heat stroke
   D. always winning

2. Ike wanted to play soccer for all of the following reasons except:
   A. awards   (B) his parents
   C. fame   D. money

3. An antonym of the word "resume" is:
   A. continue   B. fail
   C. erupt   (D) stop

4. Coach Bull finally decides to play Ike because:
   A. Ike was the best player on the team.
   (B) All the other players had collapsed and were in the locker room.
   C. Ike's parents had persuaded the coach to play Ike.
   D. The team members persuaded the coach to play Ike.

5. "... the artificial coolness of the locker room" is just another way of saying:
   A. The locker room was underground.
   B. The locker room just seemed to be cool.
   (C) The locker room had air conditioning.
   D. The locker room had solar panels.

6. "Pow! Lights flashed like some mad carnival." When this happens in the story:
   A. Ike suddenly realizes what he must do, and he kicks the ball.
   B. Lightning strikes the light post on the soccer field.
   C. The soccer ball hits the light post and breaks the light.
   (D) Ike hits his head on the goal post and knocks himself unconscious.

Total Problems: _____ Total Correct: _____ Score: _____ **27**

28

Anyone Sitting Here?

Name _____

Read the passage and answer the questions on the following page.

Anyone Sitting Here?

One day at the movies, my mother embarrassed herself so badly that neither she nor I can ever forget that boisterously entertaining incident. The rain was pouring that day, and the thunder was loud and crashing. She and I thought it was a perfect day for a movie.

After we decided which movie we wanted to see, we dressed and headed for Albertville. The rain seemed to come down harder and faster the closer we came to our destination. Finally, after driving at a much slower speed than usual, we arrived at the theater only to find that we were late.

Disregarding the fact that we had missed five minutes of the opening scene, we purchased tickets and went into the theater. Finding a seat in a dark theater is always a difficult task, but we were anxious to get settled because we really wanted to see this show. Our eyes had not quite adjusted to the darkness, but I tried to follow my mother as she somewhat blindly looked for two seats.

She went to the middle of the theater and began to move down a row where she thought there were two empty seats. The next thing that I saw, however dark, was the figure of my mother sitting down, right into a spot where there was no seat. For whatever reason, the seat had been removed. So instead of sitting down into a seat, my mom was sprawled on the floor. Trying to maintain herself, my mom whispered loudly, "Hope, help me. I can't get up." It seemed that one of her legs had managed to get caught under the seat in front of her, and she was tugging and sighing as she tried to free it, while I giggled without restraint at the predicament my mom was in. After a minute, it seemed, my mom was free and standing, and fortunately the lights were out, because she was terribly embarrassed.

My mother and I finally located two empty seats about four rows back and proceeded to watch the movie, amidst a few silent giggles and whispers. On the way home that afternoon, my mother made me promise not to tell Dad about her disconcerting adventure that day. I did keep the promise for one hour, but it was just too funny not to tell.

Name _____   Anyone Sitting Here?

Read each question. Circle the letter beside the correct answer.

1. Where did the story take place?
   A. beach
   B. city
   C. theater *(circled)*
   D. school

2. What is the funny incident that happened in the story?
   A. The mother only wore one earring and two different colored shoes.
   B. The narrator's mother missed her chair and sat on the floor.
   C. The mother fell out of her seat onto the floor.
   D. By mistake the mother sat down into a space where a seat had been removed. *(circled)*

3. What did the mother make the narrator promise?
   A. not to tell the narrator's dad about the incident *(circled)*
   B. not to tell anyone about the incident
   C. not to tell the narrator's dad they went to Albertville
   D. not to tell the doctor they had left the house

4. In the last paragraph, another word for "disconcerting" is:
   A. flirtatious
   B. embarrassing *(circled)*
   C. musical
   D. serious

5. Number the phrases from the passage in sequential order.

A. __3__ . . . we were anxious to get settled because we really wanted to see this show.

B. __1__ . . . the thunder was loud and crashing.

C. __4__ Our eyes had not quite adjusted to the darkness, as I tried to follow . . .

D. __2__ The rain seemed to come down harder and faster . . .

E. __6__ . . . my mother made me promise not to tell Dad . . .

F. __5__ Trying to maintain herself, my mom whispered loudly, "Hope, help me."

Total Problems: _____ Total Correct: _____ Score: _____   **29**

© Carson-Dellosa CD-2206

Name _____   A Funny Sight

Read the passage and answer the questions on the following page.

A Funny Sight

The weather report for that humid July summer night wasn't that kind, but we had been planning this trip for a long time. So we decided to go ahead with our camping trip. My big brother Scott and I had chosen a perfect spot on the side of the mountain, not thinking that if it did storm, we might get drenched.

Scott had settled on his air mattress, and I was on my sleeping bag. Both of us were fast asleep when the fun began. We had been sleeping maybe about one hour when we were awakened by the storm. I said, "Scott, listen to that storm. I bet it's gonna be a gully washer. It's a good thing we dug that drainage ditch around the tent."

"Jay, we'll be fine. Go back to sleep," Scott said assuringly. My big brother was in the twelfth grade, and everyone liked him, especially me. In many ways, he was my hero, and I would do anything for him, and he would do the same for me.

About thirty minutes later, the rain was falling in torrents, and the tent was rocking, while the trees cracked and groaned in the wind. I couldn't sleep; all I could do was lie there and listen. Looking and feeling around with my small flashlight, I yelled, "Scott, there is water coming in our tent." At first, he didn't appear to hear me, so I nudged him and repeated it.

This time Scott jumped up and unzipped the tent and hurried outside. He had his floodlight with him and both of us could see our immediate area. It was then that I noticed that there was a big puddle of water beginning to form in our tent. As I pulled back the flap of the tent, I saw one of the funniest sights I have seen in a while. My brother in his purple-leopard boxer shorts was busy digging frantically around the drainage ditch with an old army shovel that our dad had given us. The sight of him standing there with rain pouring all over him and yelling for me to come out and help him made me laugh out loud. I couldn't stop laughing as I stumbled out to help him.

After some time we widened and cleared the drainage ditch around our tent, but the water inside the tent was another story. My sleeping bag was soaking wet, and Scott's air mattress was floating by now. Even Scott laughed when he saw this.

We grabbed our things and decided to move around the mountain to a pavilion that we had seen earlier that afternoon on our trek up the mountain. We thought we could sleep on the picnic table that was under the pavilion.

As we once again settled down to try to get some sleep, Scott developed a thirst for a soda, so both of us decided to get up and have sodas. We ended up talking and drinking sodas for the rest of the night, probably until around 5 o'clock in the morning. But that was great with me, because I always like hanging out with my big brother.

30

© Carson-Dellosa CD-2206

Name _____   A Funny Sight

Read each question. Circle the letter beside the correct answer.

1. The following statements about the weather are false except which one?
   A. The day had been humid, but no one suspected any bad weather.
   B. It was a typical summer night, and they were sure the weather would be good.
   C. It was raining very hard before they left their home that day.
   D. Scott and Jay knew that the weather might be bad before they left home. *(circled)*

2. The "funny sight" mentioned in the story was:
   A. Jay digging around in the rain in his purple-leopard boxer shorts.
   B. Scott running around in the rain in his paisley-leopard boxer shorts.
   C. Scott digging around in the rain in his purple-leopard boxer shorts. *(circled)*
   D. the rain coming in the tent and soaking everything Jay and Scott took with them

3. A word that means the same as "trek" is:
   A. tricked
   B. hike *(circled)*
   C. picnic
   D. quarrel

4. Which one of the following events happened first in the story?
   A. . . . Scott jumped up and unzipped the tent and hurried outside.
   B. We ended up talking and drinking sodas for the rest of the night . . .
   C. Both of us were fast asleep when the fun began. *(circled)*
   D. Looking and feeling around with my small flashlight, I yelled, . . .

5. The expression "gully washer" means:
   A. a lot of rain *(circled)*
   B. a part on cars to wash the windshields
   C. to dig a drain
   D. a light rain

6. Scott and Jay did all the following during the night except:
   A. They did get some sleep before the onslaught of the rain.
   B. Scott used his flashlight, but Jay didn't have a light to use. *(circled)*
   C. They talked and drank sodas during a big part of the night.
   D. They dug a drain around the tent before they went to sleep.

7. Another word for "pavilion" is:
   A. truck   B. mall
   C. umbrella   D. shelter *(circled)*

Total Problems: _____ Total Correct: _____ Score: _____   **31**

© Carson-Dellosa CD-2206

Name _____   The Best Christmas

Read the passage and answer the questions on the following page.

The Best Christmas

Sheila slowly glanced around the dull hospital room. A large green wreath hung on the door. Numerous Christmas cards were displayed on the two bedside tables.

"Mommy?" Jacob's tiny voice squeaked.

"Yes, dear?" Sheila asked, as she walked to the bed where her seven-year-old son lay.

"I finished my letter to Santa," Jacob stated with excitement. He then proudly held it up for his mother to see.

"You've done a great job, Jacob," Sheila responded, as she silently read Jacob's letter. The letter read: *Dear Santa, All I want for Christmas is to get better and go home. I have been good. Thanks, Jacob*

Sheila blinked back the tears as she handed the letter back to her son. It hurt her so much to see him suffering this way. "You know, Jacob, sometimes Santa isn't able to bring us everything we want," she tried to explain without being so pessimistic.

"Yes, I know, Mom, but I've been really good this year," he replied with such confidence.

"That's true," his mother agreed. It seemed as though Jacob had been too sick and weak to misbehave. Suddenly, a knock was heard on the door and Dr. Clarke, the hospital's neurologist, entered the room without waiting for a response. "Hi there, Jacob," he said with a kind and sincere tone. "How have you been feeling?"

"A lot better," Jacob answered with a smile.

"Good, good fellow," Dr. Clarke replied, while listening to Jacob's heart with his stethoscope. He then turned to Sheila and said, "May I see you in the hall for a minute?"

"Sure," Sheila replied apprehensively. The two exited the room and Jacob continued to read and look at his letter.

"Mrs. Lang," the doctor began, "the results from Jacob's last biopsy have come back." Sheila's face froze and she was speechless. "The tests show that the tumor has completely disappeared, and there are no signs of cancerous cells in any of the surrounding areas. It looks as if the chemotherapy has worked. The disease is in remission." We will need to check him again in a month to make sure the tumor doesn't return but it should be okay for him to go home for the holidays."

Sheila hardly knew what to do. Should she cry or should she laugh for joy? After all this time, she couldn't believe that Jacob's cancer was finally gone. A rush of happiness flooded her body. Then, she spoke, "Thank you, Dr. Clarke. Thank you so very much."

"I am pleased to give this information to you," the doctor replied. "We can have a meeting with the staff in the next two days and discuss Jacob's outpatient care plan. But, for now, why don't you go in and tell him the good news?"

"Okay, I will," Sheila responded with a happiness she had never felt in her life. "Thank you again, Dr. Clarke. You don't know how much this means to Jacob and our family."

Sheila opened the door to her son's hospital room and entered. She couldn't wait to tell Jacob the good news that his Christmas wish was going to come true after all.

32

© Carson-Dellosa CD-2206

Name _____   The Best Christmas

Read each question. Circle the letter beside the correct answer.

1. The main idea of this story is:
   A. There are good doctors everywhere.
   B. Spending the holiday in a hospital would be pleasant.
   C. Sometimes wishes come true.
   D. A parent cannot be taken for granted.

2. What did Jacob want for Christmas?
   A. a new computer
   B. to get better and go home
   C. a private room
   D. a new doctor

3. "The tests show that the tumor has completely disappeared, and there are no signs of cancerous cells in any of the surrounding areas. It looks as if the chemotherapy has worked. The disease is in remission." Which is *not* a context clue for the meaning of the word remission?
   A. the tumor has completely disappeared,
   B. there are no signs of cancerous cells
   C. any of the surrounding areas
   D. the chemotherapy has worked

4. "You know, Jacob, sometimes Santa isn't able to bring us everything we want," she tried to explain without being so pessimistic. What inference can be made by Sheila's comment to her son Jacob?
   A. She is trying to prepare her son for disappointment in case he does not get better and cannot go home.
   B. She is trying to tell Jacob there is no Santa Claus.
   C. She is trying to tell Jacob that their family does not have much money.
   D. She is trying to tell Jacob that he wants too much.

5. Another word or expression that means the same as "remission" is:
   A. coma
   B. free from symptoms
   C. terminally ill
   D. anxiety

6. Which event happened last?
   A. He then proudly held it up for this mother to see.
   B. A rush of happiness flooded her body.
   C. Sheila told Dr. Clarke, "You don't know how much this means to Jacob and our family."
   D. "Hi there, Jacob," he said with a kind and sincere tone.

© Carson-Dellosa CD-2206

| Total Problems: | Total Correct: | Score: |

33

Name _____   Swimming with Nurse Sharks

Read the passage and answer the questions on the following page.

Swimming with Nurse Sharks

This summer my dad and I shared an experience that I will never forget. We went scuba diving in the crystal blue waters of the Gulf of Mexico. My mom and brother missed this exploration because my brother had a golf tournament in Birmingham. My mom decided to accompany Brax to the tournament, so my vacation became a father-daughter one. Saddened that this would not be another memorable family vacation, I was still excited about my first saltwater dive, and being able to share this experience with my dad only made it more special.

The boat was rocking and my nerves were running wild as we approached the oil rig. Then, suddenly, I became sick. One of the crew members tried to calm my nerves while the other one told my dad that I was sick. No matter what the crew members did to make me feel better, nothing helped as much as a hug from my dad. I spent the rest of the ride asleep with my head on my dad's shoulder. Just knowing that my dad is always there gives me the safest feeling in the world.

Once the boat stopped, my dad's main concern was to get me into the water. As I was getting dressed, everywhere I turned my dad was there holding whatever I needed. I entered the water and waited for him. Once my dad and the dive master joined me, we began our descent. Not long after we began our descent, the dive master stopped me. Wondering why the descent had stopped, I looked around and realized that my dad was not with us. My heart started to race as I looked around for him. He was nowhere to be found. Finally, I looked up and saw two legs kicking at the surface. Lacking the proper amount of weight, he was stranded at the surface. The dive master ascended and grabbed Dad's hand and pulled him down.

Once we finished our descent, we were ready to explore. I had never realized how vast the ocean was until I was really in it. I felt a little insignificant, like a grain of sand in the Sahara Desert. However, knowing that my dad was there with me made this feeling go away. We had been swimming around at a depth of sixty feet for about fifteen minutes when dad informed me that he was low on air. He returned to the surface. With a sufficient air supply, the dive master and I decided to continue our dive at twenty feet.

Swimming around the oil rig, I saw a mysterious dark figure in the distance. Swimming closer, I struggled to make out the shapes: a long, light brown tail and a dorsal fin. Then it moved and I noticed it was a shark. My heart started to pound, as I realized that four or five sharks surrounded me. Meticulously studying the sharks, I realized they were only nurse sharks and practically harmless. I swam around to get a closer look at one of the shark's faces. It had a kind, yet mysterious, look in its eyes. I failed to see how someone could perceive this to be a life-threatening animal.

I hated to call this perfect dive to a halt, but my air supply was running low. Seeing a shark on my first saltwater dive was an experience that I will never forget. I couldn't wait to tell my mom and brother about this unbelievable experience. I wished this could have been another one of our unforgettable family vacations, but my brother placed in the golf tournament so the separation was worthwhile this time. Furthermore, scuba diving in the Gulf of Mexico was the best father-daughter vacation I could have ever imagined.

34

© Carson-Dellosa CD-2206

Name _____   Swimming with Nurse Sharks

Read each question. Circle the letter beside the correct answer.

1. The story is mainly about:
   A. snorkeling in the Gulf of Mexico
   B. swimming with nurse sharks in the Gulf of Mexico
   C. a family of four who enjoy a vacation together in the Gulf of Mexico
   D. sharing a special vacation experience with a dad

2. In the fourth paragraph, the narrator compares herself to a grain of sand in the Sahara Desert. This comparison between the narrator and sand is called a:
   A. metaphor
   B. simile
   C. pun
   D. paradox

3. Another word or expression that means the same as meticulously is:
   A. approximately
   B. carefully
   C. not precisely
   D. haphazardly

4. Why didn't the narrator's brother go scuba diving?
   A. He preferred to sun on the beach instead.
   B. He went deep-sea fishing with his mother.
   C. He attended a golf tournament in Birmingham.
   D. He stayed home to study for a summer school exam.

5. Upon their initial descent into the water, the dad becomes stranded because:
   A. He was scared and didn't want to go any further.
   B. Suddenly he was sick and fatigued.
   C. He lacked the proper amount of weight.
   D. He saw a shark in the distance.

6. What happened last in the story?
   A. The boat was rocking and my nerves were running wild as we approached the oil rig.
   B. Swimming around the oil rig, I saw a mysterious dark figure in the distance.
   C. The divemaster ascended and grabbed Dad's hand and pulled him down.
   D. . . . my brother placed in the golf tournament so the separation was worthwhile . . .

© Carson-Dellosa CD-2206

| Total Problems: | Total Correct: | Score: |

35

Name _____   The Last Game

Read the passage and answer the questions on the following page.

The Last Game

It was the beginning of the end. The final football game had just begun. As a senior, Michelle Rogers was cheering her last football game. She was so excited, but yet so sad. Her cheering career would be over in four quarters.

All the cheerleaders, including Michelle, were lined up ready to cheer the team. This game was not only the last game of the year but also the most important game. Michelle's team, the Greenwood Knights, were facing the undefeated Gunter Wildcats. The teams were lined up, ready to run onto the field. The band started playing and both teams ran out. The fans were ecstatic!

The kickoff was about to begin. Michelle was so excited. The kick was absolutely the greatest, and the fans went crazy. The announcer was talking about all the fans and the excitement of the game. Led by Michelle, the cheerleaders had a great cheer at all times.

Suddenly, it was already halftime, and the score was 14-7, with Gunter leading. Michelle wanted her Knights to win. Her voice was almost gone from cheering her team on for the first half of the game. The second half would be even worse because the score was so close.

When the second half started, both teams were really excited. Michelle wondered what the coach could have said to the players in the locker room. After cheering long and hard, it was finally down to the last quarter with one minute to go, and the score was 14-14.

Michelle was ecstatic! Greenwood had the ball at the 50-yard line. For a second, she wandered away in her own world—thinking about her past football games. Suddenly, she was awakened from her momentary daydreaming by a friend screaming at her that they had won the game. The crowd was going crazy.

As Michelle joined the crowd's spirit and vivacity, she again flashed back through four years of fun games and sportsmanship. She remembered the winning games, and she also remembered the losing games. However, she would always remember this night because it seemed a perfect ending to a perfect season.

36

© Carson-Dellosa CD-2206

© Carson-Dellosa CD-2206

Name _____ The Last Game

Read each question. Circle the letter beside the correct answer.

1. One main idea of this story is:
   A. The Gunter Wildcats always beat the Greenwood Knights.
   B. Michelle Rogers was cheering her last football game.
   C. Sports events can be exciting and provide a lot of great memories.
   D. Baseball is a very tough sport.

2. At halftime, who was winning the game?
   A. Michelle
   B. Gunter
   C. Greenwood
   D. Stewart

3. Which one of the following events occurred last?
   A. As Michelle joined the crowd's spirit and vivacity, she again flashed . . .
   B. . . . she was awakened from her momentary daydreaming by a friend . . .
   C. . . . it was down to the last quarter with one minute to go, . . .
   D. The teams were lined up ready to begin their game.

4. Another word that means the same as the word "ecstatic" is:
   A. overwhelmed
   B. unruly
   C. angry
   D. moody

5. Michelle was awakened from her daydreaming by:
   A. the loud noise of the crowd, jumping and screaming
   B. a friend screaming at her
   C. her mother screaming that breakfast was ready
   D. her teacher telling her to wake up and do her work

6. Which one of the following statements is not true?
   A. Tonight was the last game of the season.
   B. At halftime, Greenwood was losing the game.
   C. Gunter had only lost one game this year prior to the game with Greenwood.
   D. Gunter lost the game with Greenwood.

7. A word that has the opposite meaning of the word "vivacity" is:
   A. happiness   B. sensitivity
   C. inanimate   D. joy

© Carson-Dellosa CD-2206

| Total Problems: | Total Correct: | Score: |

37

Name _____ Good Business Sense

Read the following passage and answer the questions on the following page.

Good Business Sense

Brad slowly sipped his scalding coffee as he watched the glossy California sun come up over the seemingly never-ending Pacific Ocean. Brad Stewart was about to embark on one of the most important and most memorable days of his life. Today was the grand opening of Brad's new business. He had graduated last year from the University of Southern California with a degree in business.

The plan for Stewart's Software Company had been in the making for almost a year now. While Brad had been working with a larger company, he had been gathering information for what was needed to create and manage a new, up-and-coming business. A building had already been purchased 34 days ago and had been renovated with offices, warehouse, and retail floor space. Loans had been made from the bank as well as from Brad's parents. Finally, the day had arrived.

The store was set to make its opening at eight o'clock. Brad was there early enough to make sure everything went smoothly. By the time the doors were open, several customers were waiting in line to enter. At eight o'clock sharp when Brad unlocked the automatic door and stepped in front of it to open, nothing happened. The same thing had happened with the door the day before, but Brad knew exactly what to do. Quickly he ran upstairs, adjusted the automatic electric eye switch, and then rushed back downstairs. He waved to the customers outside and stepped again in front of the door. It worked and the people rushed in as kids would to the grand opening of a new toy store. It seemed as if not one customer left the store empty-handed. The first day didn't seem to have enough hours before the closing hour of five o'clock. Brad's smile seemed to stay intact throughout the day and seemed to get even larger as he calculated the business from the first day.

The first day's income was enough to make a substantial dent in Brad's loans. Moreover, he was able to make his loans disappear within the first three months of business. Now, three years later, Brad runs a large chain of stores in northern California and is considered one of the most successful businessmen in the state.

38

© Carson-Dellosa CD-2206

Name _____ Good Business Sense

Read each question. Circle the letter beside the correct answer.

1. What happened on the day the store was set to open?
   A. The grand opening of a new toy store took place.
   B. Brad opened the door at eight o'clock sharp to greet the customers.
   C. The automatic door would not open.
   D. Brad graduated from the University of Southern California.

2. Another word that means the same as intact is:
   A. covered
   B. whole
   C. twisted
   D. broken

3. How much money did Brad make the first day his store opened?
   A. enough money to pay off much of his debt
   B. not much money at all
   C. enough money to pay off all of his debt
   D. no money at all

4. The setting for "Good Business Sense" is:
   A. southern California
   B. Pacific Ocean
   C. northern California
   D. Oregon

5. Brad graduated with a degree in:
   A. English
   B. law
   C. mathematics
   D. business

6. A word that means the opposite of the word "substantial" is:
   A. above   B. insignificant
   C. underground   D. great

7. One might decide the main idea of the story is:
   A. to always make sure the door is working properly before scheduling a grand opening
   B. that everyone should graduate from a university or college
   C. that one should never make loans from a bank or lending institution
   D. that with hard work and perseverance a person can become successful

© Carson-Dellosa CD-2206

| Total Problems: | Total Correct: | Score: |

39

Name _____ Angel's Punishment

Read the passage and answer the questions that follow. Circle the letter beside the correct answer.

Angel's Punishment

As he was coming down for breakfast, young Angel tripped and bruised his knee. As if this were not bad enough, he had also forgotten to do his book report that was due today in seventh grade English. When his mother asked him if he had finished his report, he said that he had, but she could not see it because he had saved it onto a disk.

Arriving at school, Angel's stomach had more butterflies than a field in early spring. He desperately wanted to get some sort of grade so he thought that if he told his teacher a little white lie he might make something positive out of the situation. When his teacher asked him for his report, he told her that while he was finishing his report, his computer crashed. He begged his teacher for one more day to get it to her. Since Angel had always been a satisfactory student, she decided to allow him another day to get the report to her. After this encounter, the rest of school that day was good.

When the last bell rang for school to end, Angel hurried home to get an early start on his report. Before he was ten feet into his room, his mother called him into the kitchen. She wanted to know what grade he had gotten on his report. He told her that the reports had not been graded yet. When she heard this, his mother became very upset. She said the teacher had called to say how sorry she felt that Angel's computer had crashed and that she was allowing him to turn in the report tomorrow. Angel's stomach hit the floor. With his desperate lies, he had put himself into a web of tangled stories.

After the whole truth was revealed, Angel finished his report on paper, because his computer had been taken away for one week. The report was ten pages handwritten, and it took him three hours to do it, whereas on his computer he could have done it in half the time.

1. The main idea of this story is:
   A. Doing homework on the computer is simpler than writing it by hand.
   B. It is all right to stretch the truth just a little.
   C. It is not so bad to put off doing assignments until the last minute.
   D. It is always best to tell the truth.

2. In the second paragraph, the expression "Angel's stomach had more butterflies than a field in early spring" means:
   A. Angel ate some bad food for breakfast.
   B. Angel is very nervous about the report.
   C. Angel probably has had a stomach operation recently.
   D. Angel saw butterflies in a field on his way to school.

40

| Total Problems: | Total Correct: | Score: |

© Carson-Dellosa CD-2206

Name _____   Prague: City of a Hundred Spires

Read the passage and answer the questions that follow. Fill in each blank with the correct answer.

Prague: City of a Hundred Spires

Prague, the capital and largest city of the Czech Republic, lies on both sides of the banks of the Vltava River. Because of its many Gothic churches, it has been called the "City of a Hundred Spires." The city is still recovering from communism, which was expelled in 1989 during the Velvet Revolution. Student protests and marches started the anti-communist revolt that led to the entire city supporting the students' cause.

The Old Town, which served as the seat of government for hundreds of years, lies on the right bank of the Vltava River. Here one can see the Tyn Church and the prestigious Charles University, the oldest in central Europe. The university was established by Charles IV of Bohemia, who was responsible for Prague's "Golden Era," which made the city a cultural and economic center.

Atop the highest point and overlooking the city on the left bank of the Vltava River is Prague Castle, the official residence of the president. The castle has been reconstructed many times throughout history. Its well-known Gothic spires and medieval style were the ideas of Charles IV.

Despite gradual modernization, Old Prague has retained much of its original charm and appearance, with narrow streets and many historic buildings in the Gothic style. Palaces of the old nobility now house government offices and embassies. Prague suffered little damage in World War II and has approximately 1,700 officially designated historic monuments. Prague still remains a picturesque and richly historic city.

1. On the left bank, atop the highest point, is ___Prague Castle___, the official residence of the president.

2. Prague lies on both sides of the banks of the ___Vltava___ River.

3. ___Charles IV of Bohemia___ established the oldest university in central Europe and made the city a cultural and economic center.

4. Because of its many ___Gothic___ churches, Prague has been called the "City of a Hundred Spires."

5. Prague is still recovering from communism, which was expelled in ___1989___. (year)

Total Problems:	Total Correct:	Score:

© Carson-Dellosa CD-2206   **41**

Name _____   Bangkok: "The City of Angels"

Read the passage and answer the questions that follow. Fill in each blank with the correct answer.

Bangkok: "The City of Angels"

Bangkok, the capital and chief port of Thailand, is one of the most important cities in Southeast Asia. It is located on the east bank of the Chao Phraya River, which runs through the city, and is called Krung Thep, or "City of Angels," by the Thai people. Perhaps this modern city's most distinctive features are the approximately 400 Buddhist temples, called "wats." Nearly all of Thailand's citizens are Buddhist.

In smaller villages, many Thai people still live traditionally near the river. The Thai people build wooden houses that stand on stilts in the water. Boats service the houses along the way—bus boats, mail boats, and even ice cream boats stop at the houses which are entered on long, wooden planks. Although Bangkok still has many of these canal dwellings, most people in the city now live in modern apartment buildings.

Although Thai customs and etiquette have generally developed in Western fashion, take note of the following. When traveling in Thailand: (1) Avoid discussing the heads of state and the royal family in a manner that might be interpreted as demeaning or condescending. Thai have a deep love and respect for their monarch. (2) Show respect toward temples, wats and shrines, and all Buddhist images. Women must neither sit next to nor touch a monk. If a female has to hand a monk something, she should pass it to a man to hand to the monk, or place the object on a table or on the floor. (3) The head is the highest and most respected, sacred part of the body; the foot is the lowest. Do not touch a Thai on the head. Do not sit with your feet pointed at a Thai; this is a show of gross disrespect. Do not even use your feet to point at an object, such as luggage. When entering a Thai home or a temple, remove your shoes. Never lose your temper—you will lose the respect and goodwill of all watching.

1. There are nearly 400 Buddhist temples, called ___wats___, in Bangkok.

2. The Thai people have a deep love and respect for their ___monarch___.

3. What is the meaning of *Krung Thep*? ___City of Angels___.

4. The ___Chao Praya___ River, located on the east bank, flows through Bangkok.

5. It is customary among Thai that women must neither sit next to nor touch a ___monk___.

42 | Total Problems: | Total Correct: | Score: | © Carson-Dellosa CD-2206

Name _____   Cape Town, South Africa

Read the passage and answer the questions that follow. Circle the letter beside the correct answer.

Cape Town, South Africa

Cape Town, first called Cape of Good Hope, is the legislative capital and the largest and most scenic city of South Africa. Situated on Table Bay at the foot of Table Mountain, a national landmark, and overlooking the Atlantic Ocean, Cape Town was colonized by European settlers. Its climate is typically Mediterranean—winters are cool and wet, and summers are warm and dry.

Cape Town was founded in 1652 by Jan van Riebeeck to serve as a supply station for the Dutch East India Company. In 1795 it was captured by a British force, but was returned to the Dutch by the Treaty of Amiens in 1803. In 1806 it again came under British control. Following the discovery of diamonds in 1867 and gold in 1886 in the interior, Cape Town became one of the country's largest ports and rail terminals. The Europeans of South Africa created the apartheid policy to assure that they, not the South African non-whites, would have continued economic and social control. In 1991 the laws of apartheid were abolished. In 1994, Nelson Mandela was elected the first democratic president of South Africa.

The city center focuses on the Public Gardens, a remnant of the original settlement, and on the Houses of Parliament. The Castle, begun in 1666 and completed in 1677, was a seat of government in the 17th century and is now a museum. Cape Town is the headquarters of several banks and insurance companies, and has theaters, museums, and an orchestra. It has two universities: the University of the Western Cape and the University of Cape Town. With so many attractions, it is no wonder that Cape Town continues to be a popular tourist site.

1. Cape Town was founded in 1652 to serve as:
   A. national landmark
   Ⓑ supply station for the Dutch East India Company
   C. headquarters for several banks
   D. country's largest port and rail terminal

2. The Europeans of South Africa created the apartheid policy. Apartheid means:
   Ⓐ social and economic discrimination against non-whites
   B. social and economic discrimination against whites
   C. the discovery of diamonds and gold in South Africa
   D. the control over ports and railways in South Africa

3. In 1994, who was elected as the democratic president of South Africa?
   A. Jan van Riebeeck
   B. Mandela Amiens
   C. Nelson Hope
   Ⓓ Nelson Mandela

© Carson-Dellosa CD-2206 | Total Problems: | Total Correct: | Score: | **43**

Name _____   Albert Einstein

Read the passage and answer the questions that follow. Follow the directions and circle the letter beside the correct answer.

Albert Einstein: Person of the Century

The German-American physicist, Albert Einstein, contributed more than any other scientist to the 20th-century vision of physical reality. Following World War I, his theories—especially his theory of relativity—seemed to point to a pure quality of human thought. The theory is written in the formula $E = mc^2$, which shows how space, time, and gravity are related. The E stands for energy; the m stands for mass; the c^2 stands for the velocity of light, squared.

Einstein's parents, who were Jewish, moved from Ulm to Munich, Germany when Einstein was an infant. The family business was the manufacturing of electrical apparatus. When the business failed in 1894, the family moved to Milan, Italy. At this time, Einstein decided officially to relinquish his German citizenship.

He spent the next years in Europe. He wrote academic papers and held various positions which included: a post at the Swiss patent office in Bern, where he completed an astonishing range of publications in theoretical physics; lecturer at the University of Bern; associate professor of physics at the University of Zurich; professorships at the German University of Prague and at the Zurich Polytechnic; and cross-appointment at the University of Berlin.

The Nobel Prize was awarded to Einstein in 1921 for his work on the photoelectric effect, which explains the absorption and release of energy by certain atoms by incandescent bodies. Einstein remained on the staff of the University of Berlin until 1933. With the rise of fascism in Germany, Einstein moved to the United States in 1933, where he held an analogous research position at the Institute for Advanced Study in Princeton, New Jersey. In 1939, Einstein sent the famous letter to President Franklin D. Roosevelt that urged the United States to develop an atomic bomb before Germany. However, Einstein was a strong advocate of world peace. Because of his many scientific contributions, *TIME* magazine has honored Albert Einstein as the Person of the Century. Einstein died in 1955.

1. What is the name of Einstein's famous theory?
   A. Theory of Physical Reality   B. Theory of Physics
   C. Theory of Human Thought   Ⓓ Theory of Relativity

2. In what country was Einstein born?
   A. United States   B. Israel
   Ⓒ Germany   D. Switzerland

3. Einstein won the Nobel Prize in 1921 for his work on:
   A. The Theory of Relativity   Ⓑ The Photoelectric Effect
   C. Human Thought   D. Physical Reality

44 | Total Problems: | Total Correct: | Score: | © Carson-Dellosa CD-2206

Name _____   Mildred D. Taylor

Read the passage and answer the questions that follow. Circle the letter beside the correct answer.

Meet the Writer: Mildred D. Taylor

Born in Jackson, Mississippi, Mildred D. Taylor was educated in Toledo, Ohio. She wanted to be a cheerleader in high school but instead was an honor student, a newspaper editor, and a class officer. Every summer Mildred and her family visited Mississippi relatives, and she listened to their stories. By the time she was nine, Mildred knew that she wanted to be a writer. Ms. Taylor attended the University of Toledo and received her Master's degree at the University of Colorado School of Journalism.

Mildred Taylor began her career with the Peace Corps as an English and history teacher in Ethiopia for two years. Later she returned to the United States and was a Peace Corps recruiter. After the Peace Corps, Ms. Taylor became a study skills coordinator for the University of Colorado's Black Education Program.

In 1975, her first novel, *Song of the Trees*, introduced the Logan family to American readers and won first prize in the African-American category in a competition of children's books. *Roll of Thunder, Hear My Cry*, told by Cassie, the first person narrator, was Ms. Taylor's second novel, which won the Newberry Medal in 1977. Published in 1982, *Let the Circle Be Unbroken* continues the Logan story when Cassie is 11 and Stacey is 14. There are two additional short stories about the Logans: "Mississippi Bridge" (1987) and "The Friendship" (1990).

It is quite apparent that Ms. Taylor uses her own early life as the inspiration for her stories. In 1977, when she accepted the Newberry Award for *Roll of Thunder, Hear My Cry*, she talked about her father, who taught her a truer history of black people in the United States than she had learned in school. In all her novels, Mildred D. Taylor pulls her reader into the circle of an inspiring black family.

1. Mildred D. Taylor has written all of the following except:
    A. *Roll of Thunder, Hear My Cry*
    B. *Song of the South*
    C. *Let the Circle Be Unbroken*
    D. "Mississippi Bridge"

2. When Mildred was only nine, she wanted to become a:
    A. teacher   B. lecturer
    C. writer   D. nurse

3. In 1977, Ms. Taylor accepted the Newberry Medal for having written:
    A. "The Friendship"
    B. *Let the Circle Be Unbroken*
    C. *Song of the Trees*
    D. *Roll of Thunder, Hear My Cry*

© Carson-Dellosa CD-2206 | Total Problems: | Total Correct: | Score: | **45**

Name _____   Edgar Allan Poe

Read the passage and answer the questions that follow. Circle the letter beside the correct answer.

Edgar Allan Poe, The Father of Modern Mystery

Edgar Allan Poe was one of America's greatest poets, short-story writers, and literary critics. Poe's parents were touring actors, and both died before he was three years old. He was taken into the home of John Allan, a prosperous merchant in Richmond, Virginia. His early childhood was uneventful, although he studied for 5 years in England.

"The Raven" is Poe's best-known poem and one of the most famous works in American literature. The theme of "The Raven"—the narrator's grief over the loss of an ideal love—recurs in other works by Poe. "To Helen," "Ulalume," and "For Annie" also dramatize deep-felt loyalty to a woman who symbolizes an ideal spiritual value. These poems are noted for their subtle use of rhyme, rhythm, and symbols.

With "The Murders in Rue Morgue" and other short stories, Poe became the father of modern mystery and detective fiction. In "Sonnet to Science" and "The Valley of Unrest," Poe described man's loss of innocence and sense of wonder and beauty. In "Lenore," "Annabel Lee," and "Eldorado," he implies that only love, beauty, or aspiration can save man from despair.

Poe's most popular tales are filled with an atmosphere of the strange, the bizarre, and the terrible. Many of Poe's stories are called "moral allegories" because the theme of moral responsibility prevails in them. Perhaps Poe's best story, "The Fall of the House of Usher," deals with this theme.

Poe earned only a meager living from his writings. Still, during his short life he wrote poems and stories that have made him one of the best-known American authors.

1. According to the character sketch above, Poe wrote all of the following except:
    A. "The Fall of the House of Usher"
    B. "The Valley of Unrest"
    C. "For Alice"
    D. "The Raven"

2. Poe's most popular tales are filled with an atmosphere of:
    A. the popular, the strange, and the terrible
    B. the strange, the bizarre, and the terrible
    C. love, beauty, and aspiration
    D. innocence, wonder, and beauty

3. Poe's best-known poem and one of the most famous works in American literature is:
    A. "To Helen"
    B. "Annabel Lee"
    C. "For Annie"
    D. "The Raven"

46 | Total Problems: | Total Correct: | Score: | © Carson-Dellosa CD-2206

Name _____   Making Pizza

Read the recipe and answer the questions that follow. Circle the letter beside the correct answer.

Making Pizza

Dough Ingredients
4 cups sifted all-purpose flour
1 package dry yeast
1 cup warm (85°) water
2 tablespoons vegetable or olive oil
1 teaspoon salt

Topping Ingredients
shredded mozzarella cheese
tomato sauce
pepperoni
Italian sausage
ham
sautéed onions
black olives
anchovies
chopped mushrooms
oregano

Directions
To make pizza dough, mix the ingredients as you would to make bread. Knead the dough for about 10 minutes. Cover with a damp cloth and let rise for about 2 hours. Oil two 14-inch pizza pans. Sprinkle a little flour over them. Pat and stretch the dough in the pans, pinching up a rim around the edges to hold the filling. Prick dough in about 6 places. Preheat the oven to 400°. Brush each pizza lightly with olive oil to prevent crust from becoming soggy. Spread the pizza with your favorite cheese and tomato sauce. Add toppings as desired. Let the pizza sit for 10 minutes. Bake about 25 minutes or until light brown. Serve at once.

1. When making pizza, what is the second thing that you do?
    A. Sprinkle a little flour over all.
    B. Knead the dough for about 10 minutes.
    C. Cover with a damp cloth.
    D. Let the dough rise for about 2 hours.

2. All but one of the following items is a suggested topping:
    A. black olives
    B. mushrooms
    C. pepperoni
    D. hamburger

3. How many minutes does it take to bake the pizza?
    A. 10 minutes
    B. 25 minutes
    C. 14 minutes
    D. 400 minutes

© Carson-Dellosa CD-2206 | Total Problems: | Total Correct: | Score: | **47**

Name _____   Preparing Vegetable Soup

Read the recipe and answer the questions that follow. Circle the letter beside the correct answer.

Preparing Vegetable Soup

Ingredients
2 tablespoons of bacon fat or butter
¼ cup diced carrots
½ cup diced onions
½ cup diced celery
3 cups hot water or stock
1 cup canned tomatoes

½ cup pared, diced potatoes
1 tablespoon chopped parsley
½ teaspoon salt
¼ teaspoon pepper
1 cup chopped cabbage

Directions
Place the bacon fat or butter in a large kettle. Sauté the carrots, onions, and celery, and add them to the kettle. Add the hot water or stock, tomatoes, potatoes, parsley, salt and pepper. Cover and cook about 35 minutes. Add the cabbage and cook about 5 minutes more. Remove from heat and let stand at least 5 minutes before serving. Makes about 6 cups.

1. What is the first thing to do in preparing the vegetable soup?
    A. Cut and dice the potatoes.
    B. Chop 1 cup of cabbage.
    C. Add 3 cups of hot water.
    D. Place 2 tablespoons of fat or butter in a kettle.

2. After the fat or butter, what ingredients are added next?
    A. onions, potatoes, and tomatoes
    B. carrots, onions, and celery
    C. tomatoes, potatoes, and parsley
    D. salt and pepper

3. After all the ingredients have been added to the kettle, how much longer do you cook the vegetable soup?
    A. 30 minutes
    B. 35 minutes
    C. 5 minutes
    D. 6 minutes

4. What do you do after you have sautéed the carrots, onions, and celery?
    A. Add 1 tablespoon of chopped parsley.
    B. Add 3 cups of hot water or stock.
    C. Cook about 5 minutes.
    D. Sauté briefly in the fat or butter.

48 | Total Problems: | Total Correct: | Score: | © Carson-Dellosa CD-2206

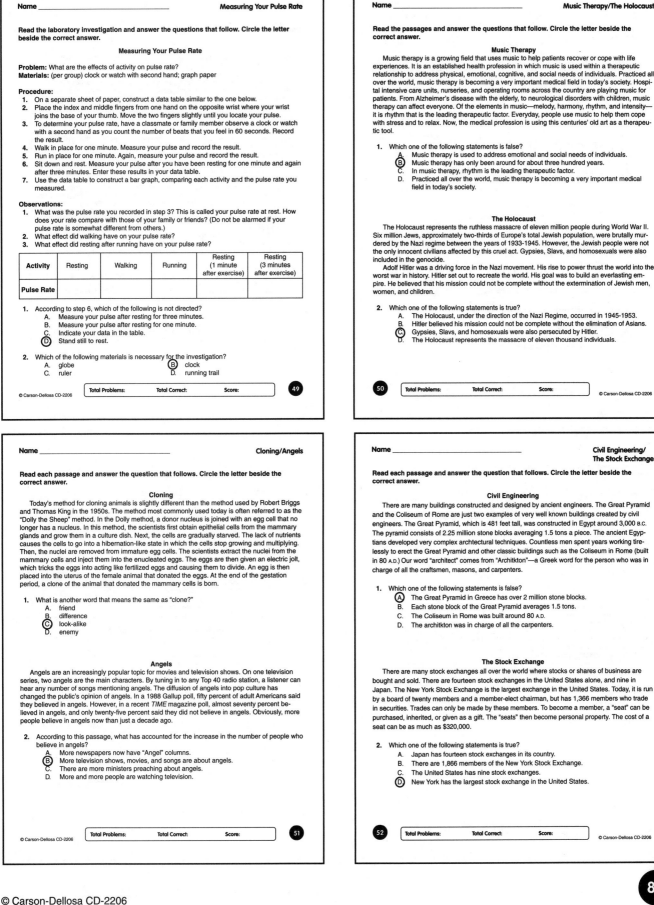

Name _____ Measuring Your Pulse Rate

Read the laboratory investigation and answer the questions that follow. Circle the letter beside the correct answer.

Measuring Your Pulse Rate

Problem: What are the effects of activity on pulse rate?
Materials: (per group) clock or watch with second hand; graph paper

Procedure:
1. On a separate sheet of paper, construct a data table similar to the one below.
2. Place the index and middle fingers from one hand on the opposite wrist where your wrist joins the base of your thumb. Move the two fingers slightly until you locate your pulse.
3. To determine your pulse rate, have a classmate or family member observe a clock or watch with a second hand as you count the number of beats that you feel in 60 seconds. Record the result.
4. Walk in place for one minute. Measure your pulse and record the result.
5. Run in place for one minute. Again, measure your pulse and record the result.
6. Sit down and rest. Measure your pulse after you have been resting for one minute and again after three minutes. Enter these results in your data table.
7. Use the data table to construct a bar graph, comparing each activity and the pulse rate you measured.

Observations:
1. What was the pulse rate you recorded in step 3? This is called your pulse rate at rest. How does your rate compare with those of your family or friends? (Do not be alarmed if your pulse rate is somewhat different from others.)
2. What effect did walking have on your pulse rate?
3. What effect did resting after running have on your pulse rate?

Activity	Resting	Walking	Running	Resting (1 minute after exercise)	Resting (3 minutes after exercise)
Pulse Rate					

1. According to step 6, which of the following is not directed?
   A. Measure your pulse after resting for three minutes.
   B. Measure your pulse after resting for one minute.
   C. Indicate your data in the table.
   D. Stand still to rest.

2. Which of the following materials is necessary for the investigation?
   A. globe   B. clock
   C. ruler   D. running trail

© Carson-Dellosa CD-2206   Total Problems:___ Total Correct:___ Score:___   **49**

Name _____ Music Therapy/The Holocaust

Read the passages and answer the questions that follow. Circle the letter beside the correct answer.

Music Therapy

Music therapy is a growing field that uses music to help patients recover or cope with life experiences. It is an established health profession in which music is used within a therapeutic relationship to address physical, emotional, cognitive, and social needs of individuals. Practiced all over the world, music therapy is becoming a very important medical field in today's society. Hospital intensive care units, nurseries, and operating rooms across the country are playing music for patients. From Alzheimer's disease with the elderly, to neurological disorders with children, music therapy can affect everyone. Of the elements in music—melody, harmony, rhythm, and intensity—it is rhythm that is the leading therapeutic factor. Everyday, people use music to help them cope with stress and to relax. Now, the medical profession is using this centuries' old art as a therapeutic tool.

1. Which one of the following statements is false?
   A. Music therapy is used to address emotional and social needs of individuals.
   B. Music therapy has only been around for about three hundred years.
   C. In music therapy, rhythm is the leading therapeutic factor.
   D. Practiced all over the world, music therapy is becoming a very important medical field in today's society.

The Holocaust

The Holocaust represents the ruthless massacre of eleven million people during World War II. Six million Jews, approximately two-thirds of Europe's total Jewish population, were brutally murdered by the Nazi regime between the years of 1933-1945. However, the Jewish people were not the only innocent civilians affected by this cruel act. Gypsies, Slavs, and homosexuals were also included in the genocide.

Adolf Hitler was a driving force in the Nazi movement. His rise to power thrust the world into the worst war in history. Hitler set out to recreate the world. His goal was to build an everlasting empire. He believed that his mission could not be complete without the extermination of Jewish men, women, and children.

2. Which one of the following statements is true?
   A. The Holocaust, under the direction of the Nazi Regime, occurred in 1945-1953.
   B. Hitler believed his mission could not be complete without the elimination of Asians.
   C. Gypsies, Slavs, and homosexuals were also persecuted by Hitler.
   D. The Holocaust represents the massacre of eleven thousand individuals.

50   Total Problems:___ Total Correct:___ Score:___   © Carson-Dellosa CD-2206

Name _____ Cloning/Angels

Read each passage and answer the question that follows. Circle the letter beside the correct answer.

Cloning

Today's method for cloning animals is slightly different than the method used by Robert Briggs and Thomas King in the 1950s. The method most commonly used today is often referred to as the "Dolly the Sheep" method. In the Dolly method, a donor nucleus is joined with an egg cell that no longer has a nucleus. In this method, the scientists first obtain epithelial cells from the mammary glands and grow them in a culture dish. Next, the cells are gradually starved. The lack of nutrients causes the cells to go into a hibernation-like state in which the cells stop growing and multiplying. Then, the nuclei are removed from immature egg cells. The scientists extract the nuclei from the mammary cells and inject them into the enucleated eggs. The eggs are then given an electric jolt, which tricks the eggs into acting like fertilized eggs and causing them to divide. An egg is then placed into the uterus of the female animal that donated the eggs. At the end of the gestation period, a clone of the animal that donated the mammary cells is born.

1. What is another word that means the same as "clone?"
   A. friend
   B. difference
   C. look-alike
   D. enemy

Angels

Angels are an increasingly popular topic for movies and television shows. On one television series, two angels are the main characters. By tuning in to any Top 40 radio station, a listener can hear any number of songs mentioning angels. The diffusion of angels into pop culture has changed the public's opinion of angels. In a 1988 Gallup poll, fifty percent of adult Americans said they believed in angels. However, in a recent *TIME* magazine poll, almost seventy percent believed in angels, and only twenty-five percent said they did not believe in angels. Obviously, more people believe in angels now than just a decade ago.

2. According to this passage, what has accounted for the increase in the number of people who believe in angels?
   A. More newspapers now have "Angel" columns.
   B. More television shows, movies, and songs are about angels.
   C. There are more ministers preaching about angels.
   D. More and more people are watching television.

© Carson-Dellosa CD-2206   Total Problems:___ Total Correct:___ Score:___   **51**

Name _____ Civil Engineering/ The Stock Exchange

Read each passage and answer the question that follows. Circle the letter beside the correct answer.

Civil Engineering

There are many buildings constructed and designed by ancient engineers. The Great Pyramid and the Coliseum of Rome are just two examples of very well known buildings created by civil engineers. The Great Pyramid, which is 481 feet tall, was constructed in Egypt around 3,000 B.C. The pyramid consists of 2.25 million stone blocks averaging 1.5 tons a piece. The ancient Egyptians developed very complex archtectural techniques. Countless men spent years working tirelessly to erect the Great Pyramid and other classic buildings such as the Coliseum in Rome (built in 80 A.D.) Our word "architect" comes from "Archittkton"—a Greek word for the person who was in charge of all the craftsmen, masons, and carpenters.

1. Which one of the following statements is false?
   A. The Great Pyramid in Greece has over 2 million stone blocks.
   B. Each stone block of the Great Pyramid averages 1.5 tons.
   C. The Coliseum in Rome was built around 80 A.D.
   D. The architkton was in charge of all the carpenters.

The Stock Exchange

There are many stock exchanges all over the world where stocks or shares of business are bought and sold. There are fourteen stock exchanges in the United States alone, and nine in Japan. The New York Stock Exchange is the largest stock exchange in the United States. Today, it is run by a board of twenty members and a member-elect chairman, but has 1,366 members who trade in securities. Trades can only be made by these members. To become a member, a "seat" can be purchased, inherited, or given as a gift. The "seats" then become personal property. The cost of a seat can be as much as $320,000.

2. Which one of the following statements is true?
   A. Japan has fourteen stock exchanges in its country.
   B. There are 1,866 members of the New York Stock Exchange.
   C. The United States has nine stock exchanges.
   D. New York has the largest stock exchange in the United States.

52   Total Problems:___ Total Correct:___ Score:___   © Carson-Dellosa CD-2206

Name _____

Wildlife Conservation/
History of Basketball

Read each passage and answer the question that follows. Circle the letter beside the correct answer.

Wildlife Conservation

Convinced of the enormous destructive power of human kind, pioneer conservationists of the early twentieth century emphasized the ethical responsibility of their own generation to conserve resources. During the past 2,000 years, the world has lost, through extinction, well over 100 species or sub-species of mammals. Approximately two-thirds of these losses have occurred since the mid-nineteenth century. Many other species are threatened in addition to those mammals that are already extinct. The primary factor in the depletion of the world's fauna has been modern human society, either directly through excessive hunting, or indirectly through destroying natural habitats.

1. Which one of the following is not a factor in the depletion of the fauna?
   A. destroying natural habitats
   B. modern human society
   C. not enough planting in the spring
   D. excessive hunting

History of Basketball

Basketball acquired its biggest boost when it was included in the 1936 Olympic Games in Berlin. Basketball had finally arrived as a major sport. From then on, scholastic, collegiate, and professional basketball grew quickly. Many organizations were created, such as the American Basketball League, The National Basketball League, and the National Basketball Association (NBA). In 1967, a professional league called the American Basketball Association was formed. It merged with the NBA in 1976, forming a twenty-two team league. During the 1970s and 1980s, college basketball greatly increased in popularity. The NCAA Division I men's championship tournament now ranks among the major sport events of the year.

2. What event caused basketball to grow and become a major sport?
   A. 1936 Olympic Games in Munich
   B. a merger with the NCAA in 1976
   C. 1936 Olympic Games in Berlin
   D. an organization created to boost basketball

| Total Problems: | Total Correct: | Score: | 53 |

© Carson-Dellosa CD-2206

Name _____

Morocco

Read the passage and answer the questions on the following page.

Morocco

Morocco, located along the Atlantic coast of Africa, measures 565 miles (910 km) from north to south and 730 miles (1,170 km) from east to west. It has 1,140 miles (1,835 km) of coastline along the North Atlantic Ocean and the Mediterranean Sea. Morocco has three main land regions: the Coastal Lowlands, the Atlas Mountain Chain, and the Sahara. Fertile plains are located in the Coastal Lowlands. The Atlas Mountain Chain crosses the middle of Morocco from southwest to northeast. East and south of the mountains lies the barren, sunbaked Sahara.

In Morocco, Arabs constitute the majority of the population, although Berbers, the original inhabitants, constitute about one-third of the people. The Berbers, who form a larger minority in Morocco than in any other North African country, are concentrated in the mountains. Arabic is the official language, but various Berber dialects continue to be spoken. French is still widely used, especially in government and business. Islam is the official religion, to which almost 99% of the inhabitants adhere. About 30,000 Jews live in Morocco, and almost all of the Europeans there are Roman Catholic.

Perhaps the most important element in Moroccan social life is the extended family. Ordinarily the household includes two parents, unmarried children, and married sons with their families. When the father dies, married sons establish their own households. Sometimes in the crowded urban areas, sons leave home before their father dies. Many of the homes consist of one large room that serves as the kitchen, living room, sleeping quarters, and barn. In the desert areas, some Moroccans are quite nomadic and live in tents. Urban dwellers often live in small attached houses. The wealthy, however, live in modern apartment buildings or spacious homes while the poor live in sprawling slums called "bidonvilles" (tin can towns) on the outskirts of large cities.

About half of Morocco's labor force is engaged in agriculture. Large, mechanized farms cover about one-third of the land presently available for cultivation and account for 85% of the total agricultural output. Wheat and barley, sugar beets, rice, and cotton constitute the chief crops for domestic consumption. Citrus fruits, winter vegetables, and grapes for wine are the principal export crops.

Popular Moroccan dishes include lemon chicken, tajine (a meat stew with vegetables), and a pastry made with honey and almonds. Mint tea is the national drink. Moroccans eat with their fingers from a large communal dish.

Moroccans wear traditional clothing although city dwellers often combine traditional garments with western-style clothing. Men wear a jellaba, a loose-fitting hooded robe with long, full sleeves. Rural men wear a burnoose, a heavier garment. Men usually wear a turban or brimless cap. Women also wear a jellaba as an outer garment. Some Islamic women still cover their face with a veil.

Elementary and secondary school is free in Morocco. For children ages seven to thirteen, school is compulsory; however, less than 70% attend. Approximately 50% of adult Moroccans are literate.

The most popular spectator sports in Morocco are soccer and basketball. Gathering at cafes as well as visiting with family are important leisure activities.

54

© Carson-Dellosa CD-2206

Name _____

Morocco

Read each question. Circle the letter beside the correct answer.

1. All of the following statements are true except:
   A. Arabic is the official language of Morocco.
   B. The poor live in duplex apartments near the wealthy class.
   C. About half of Morocco's labor force is engaged in agriculture.
   D. Elementary and secondary school is free in Morocco.

2. The most important element in Moroccan social life is the:
   A. extended family
   B. traditional clothing
   C. communal dish
   D. language

3. School is mandatory for children ages:
   A. six to thirteen
   B. five to fifteen
   C. seven to sixteen
   D. seven to thirteen

4. The chief Moroccan crops for domestic consumption are all of the following except:
   A. wheat and barley
   B. sugar beets
   C. corn
   D. cotton

5. The poor live in sprawling slums called:
   A. tajine
   B. burnoose
   C. jellaba
   D. bidonvilles

| Total Problems: | Total Correct: | Score: | 55 |

© Carson-Dellosa CD-2206

Name _____

Camouflaged

Read the poem and answer the questions on the following page.

Camouflaged

My parents don't understand me,
but they try to.

I see the trees,
but only hear the birds.

My sister says she cares,
but I can't tell.

My teachers think I am smart,
but I only do what they say.

My peers think they know me,
but do I know them?

My boyfriend and I sometimes do homework together,
but we never have real conversations.

My English class expects me to give the right answers,
but I need answers of my own.

I want to do something great,
but what's holding me back?

Sometimes I wonder who I really am.
I wonder.

56

© Carson-Dellosa CD-2206

Camouflaged

Name _____ Camouflaged

Read each question. Circle the letter beside the correct answer.

1. The word "camouflage" means:
   A. confusing
   B. open
   C. hidden
   D. provoking

2. Possibly, the main idea of this poem is:
   A. friends don't understand the speaker
   B. conflicts within the self and relationships with others
   C. wanting to do something which seems impossible
   D. feeling egotistical and self-centered

3. Possibly, another word for the word "peers" in line 9 is:
   A. siblings
   B. enemies
   C. relatives
   D. classmates

4. Which two types of imagery are presented in lines 3 and 4?
   A. sight and sound
   B. smell and feeling
   C. sight and feeling
   D. sight and smelling

5. "Sometimes I wonder who I really am," in line 17, suggests that the speaker:
   A. thinks she is adopted
   B. thinks she is doing some bad things
   C. is involved in self-reflection
   D. has had an episode of amnesia

| Total Problems: | Total Correct: | Score: | 57 |

© Carson-Dellosa CD-2206

Billy Bowman

Name _____ Billy Bowman

Read the poem and answer the questions on the following page.

Billy Bowman

One Saturday Billy Bowman was on his way
to get his fine horse some hay.
He stopped at Mrs. Bea's
for biscuits and tea.
Then he continued on his way.

Billy Bowman kept on his way
to get his fine horse some hay.
He stopped at Cindy Lou's
to watch the noontime news.
Then he continued on his way.

Billy Bowman traveled on his way
to get his fine horse some hay.
He stopped at the the Hound and the Deer
for his favorite game of billiards.
Then he continued on his way.

Billy Bowman continued on his way
to get his fine horse some hay.
He left in the morning,
traveling here and traveling there.
Then he continued on his way.

Billy Bowman bought the hay
and knew he must be on his way.
For his fine horse was a beautiful bay
out in the pasture where he lay.
Returning before sundown in the calm of the day.

58

© Carson-Dellosa CD-2206

Billy Bowman

Name _____ Billy Bowman

Read each question. Circle the letter beside the correct answer.

1. "He stopped at The Hound and Deer for his favorite game of billiards." What are the context clues that indicate what The Hound and the Deer is?
   A. "He stopped" suggests office
   B. "game of" suggests gym
   C. "billiards" suggests club
   D. "for his favorite" suggests store

2. For what purpose was Billy Bowman traveling?
   A. to see Cindy Lou
   B. to get hay for his horse
   C. to sell some of his hay
   D. to see the countryside

3. What is noticeable about lines 1, 2, and 5 in all the stanzas?
   A. pun
   B. personification
   C. simile
   D. rhyme

4. A lesson that Billy Bowman teaches concerning pets and animals is:
   A. Don't shun and ignore responsibilities.
   B. Don't have a horse as a responsibility.
   C. Don't buy biscuits from Mrs. Bea.
   D. Don't play billiards in the Hound and the Deer.

5. Why did Billy Bowman stop at Cindy Lou's?
   A. to ask her hand in marriage
   B. to watch the noontime news
   C. to get hay for his horse
   D. to play his favorite game of billiards

6. When Billy Bowman left that morning, he was "traveling here and traveling there." This line probably suggests that:
   A. He had many errands to attend to that day.
   B. He didn't know where he was going.
   C. He became lost and had a difficult time getting back home.
   D. He bought hay from several different people.

| Total Problems: | Total Correct: | Score: | 59 |

© Carson-Dellosa CD-2206

Nature Is

Name _____ Nature Is

Read the poem and answer the questions that follow. Circle the letter beside the correct answer.

Nature Is

Nature is a polar bear
running alongside her cub.
Nature is a mockingbird
singing a beautiful song.
Nature is a salmon
finding its way in the stream.

Nature is the rain
watering the earth.
Nature is the stars, the moon,
the pendulum of the seasons.
Nature is a voice.
See and know me, it cries.

Nature is beauty.
Nature is creation.

1. What is one noticeable difference between the first stanza and the second stanza?
   A. The first is about animal life, and the second is about the physical earth and universe.
   B. The first is about a fish, and the second is about a mockingbird.
   C. The first is about beauty, and the second is about creation.
   D. The first is about winds, and the second is about animals.

2. In line 10, the seasons are compared to a pendulum. This is called:
   A. metaphor
   B. alliteration
   C. simile
   D. paradox

3. The main idea of the poem is:
   A. Nature is a beautiful creation.
   B. the positive forces in nature
   C. the negative forces in nature
   D. Nature cannot be trusted anytime.

60

© Carson-Dellosa CD-2206

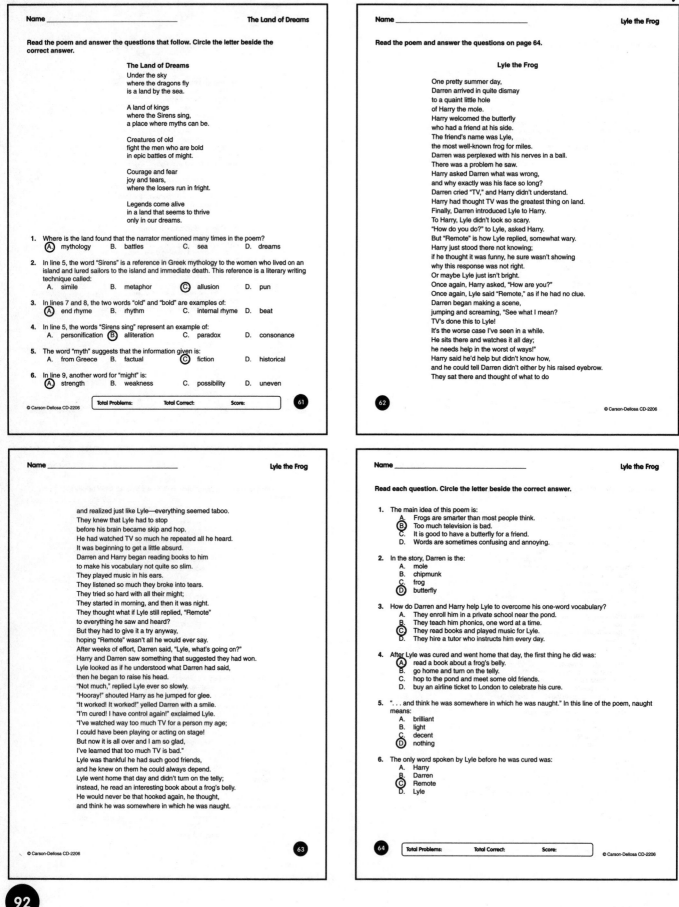

Name _____   The Land of Dreams

Read the poem and answer the questions that follow. Circle the letter beside the correct answer.

The Land of Dreams

Under the sky
where the dragons fly
is a land by the sea.

A land of kings
where the Sirens sing,
a place where myths can be.

Creatures of old
fight the men who are bold
in epic battles of might.

Courage and fear
joy and tears,
where the losers run in fright.

Legends come alive
in a land that seems to thrive
only in our dreams.

1. Where is the land found that the narrator mentioned many times in the poem?
   (A) mythology   B. battles   C. sea   D. dreams

2. In line 5, the word "Sirens" is a reference in Greek mythology to the women who lived on an island and lured sailors to the island and immediate death. This reference is a literary writing technique called:
   A. simile   B. metaphor   **(C)** allusion   D. pun

3. In lines 7 and 8, the two words "old" and "bold" are examples of:
   (A) end rhyme   B. rhythm   C. internal rhyme   D. beat

4. In line 5, the words "Sirens sing" represent an example of:
   A. personification   **(B)** alliteration   C. paradox   D. consonance

5. The word "myth" suggests that the information given is:
   A. from Greece   B. factual   **(C)** fiction   D. historical

6. In line 9, another word for "might" is:
   (A) strength   B. weakness   C. possibility   D. uneven

Total Problems:	Total Correct:	Score:

61

© Carson-Dellosa CD-2206

Name _____   Lyle the Frog

Read the poem and answer the questions on page 64.

Lyle the Frog

One pretty summer day,
Darren arrived in quite dismay
to a quaint little hole
of Harry the mole.
Harry welcomed the butterfly
who had a friend at his side.
The friend's name was Lyle,
the most well-known frog for miles.
Darren was perplexed with his nerves in a ball.
There was a problem he saw.
Harry asked Darren what was wrong,
and why exactly was his face so long?
Darren cried "TV," and Harry didn't understand.
Harry had thought TV was the greatest thing on land.
Finally, Darren introduced Lyle to Harry.
To Harry, Lyle didn't look so scary.
"How do you do?" to Lyle, asked Harry.
But "Remote" is how Lyle replied, somewhat wary.
Harry just stood there not knowing;
if he thought it was funny, he sure wasn't showing
why this response was not right.
Or maybe Lyle just isn't bright.
Once again, Harry asked, "How are you?"
Once again, Lyle said "Remote," as if he had no clue.
Darren began making a scene,
jumping and screaming, "See what I mean?
TV's done this to Lyle!
It's the worse case I've seen in a while.
He sits there and watches it all day;
he needs help in the worst of ways!"
Harry said he'd help but didn't know how,
and he could tell Darren didn't either by his raised eyebrow.
They sat there and thought of what to do

62

© Carson-Dellosa CD-2206

Name _____   Lyle the Frog

and realized just like Lyle—everything seemed taboo.
They knew that Lyle had to stop
before his brain became skip and hop.
He had watched TV so much he repeated all he heard.
It was beginning to get a little absurd.
Darren and Harry began reading books to him
to make his vocabulary not quite so slim.
They played music in his ears.
They listened so much they broke into tears.
They tried so hard with all their might;
They started in morning, and then it was night.
They thought what if Lyle still replied, "Remote"
to everything he saw and heard?
But they had to give it a try anyway,
hoping "Remote" wasn't all he would ever say.
After weeks of effort, Darren said, "Lyle, what's going on?"
Harry and Darren saw something that suggested they had won.
Lyle looked as if he understood what Darren had said,
then he began to raise his head.
"Not much," replied Lyle ever so slowly.
"Hooray!" shouted Harry as he jumped for glee.
"It worked! It worked!" yelled Darren with a smile.
"I'm cured! I have control again!" exclaimed Lyle.
"I've watched way too much TV for a person my age;
I could have been playing or acting on stage!
But now it is all over and I am so glad,
I've learned that too much TV is bad."
Lyle was thankful he had such good friends,
and he knew on them he could always depend.
Lyle went home that day and didn't turn on the telly;
instead, he read an interesting book about a frog's belly.
He would never be that hooked again, he thought,
and think he was somewhere in which he was naught.

63

© Carson-Dellosa CD-2206

Name _____   Lyle the Frog

Read each question. Circle the letter beside the correct answer.

1. The main idea of this poem is:
   A. Frogs are smarter than most people think.
   (B) Too much television is bad.
   C. It is good to have a butterfly for a friend.
   D. Words are sometimes confusing and annoying.

2. In the story, Darren is the:
   A. mole
   B. chipmunk
   C. frog
   (D) butterfly

3. How do Darren and Harry help Lyle to overcome his one-word vocabulary?
   A. They enroll him in a private school near the pond.
   B. They teach him phonics, one word at a time.
   (C) They read books and played music for Lyle.
   D. They hire a tutor who instructs him every day.

4. After Lyle was cured and went home that day, the first thing he did was:
   (A) read a book about a frog's belly.
   B. go home and turn on the telly.
   C. hop to the pond and meet some old friends.
   D. buy an airline ticket to London to celebrate his cure.

5. ". . . and think he was somewhere in which he was naught." In this line of the poem, naught means:
   A. brilliant
   B. light
   C. decent
   (D) nothing

6. The only word spoken by Lyle before he was cured was:
   A. Harry
   B. Darren
   (C) Remote
   D. Lyle

64

Total Problems:	Total Correct:	Score:

© Carson-Dellosa CD-2206

© Carson-Dellosa CD-2206

Worksheet 65 — Picture Day

Name _____ Picture Day

Read the poem and answer the questions that follow. Circle the letter beside the correct answer.

Picture Day

Picture day!
What a fun treat.
There for a five-minute deal,
and always, a thirty-five minute ordeal.

On a stool with five little ones wiggling around.
Boys in the back, pushing and jumping.
Younger girl ripping a display present
and wanting her mother.

Two older grandchildren sitting looking bored,
waiting for at least one shot.
Photographer trying to get the youngsters' attention,
and doesn't seem to get anywhere.

Standing, waiting, and wondering—
why we are here?
Grandmother, everyone knows, patiently smiling
and waiting for the picture beside her bed.

1. Everyone is having a picture taken because:
   A. They don't have one.
   B. The two older grandchildren wanted to.
   C. The grandmother wanted a photograph of her grandchildren.
   D. The grandmother was a photographer.

2. What are the two older grandchildren doing?
   A. shopping for new jeans
   B. looking bored
   C. making funny faces at everyone
   D. helping the photographer

3. Another word for ordeal is:
   A. to play cards
   B. temperament
   C. trial or test
   D. wait

© Carson-Dellosa CD-2206

Total Problems: Total Correct: Score: **65**

Worksheet 66 — Spring Song

Name _____ Spring Song

Read the poem and each question that follows. Circle the letter beside the correct answer.

Spring Song

Oh, what a glorious feeling to
step into that world of spring!
Burdens and responsibilities are
lifted from shoulders that can hold no more
and spring assaults the senses.

Eyes delight in the blossoming cherry tree
whose boughs gently sway in the cool breeze.
Lying on my back, I look up at the blue sky
where clouds gather like dreams
having taken flight from my mind.

Smells of freshly mowed grass are the
sweetest perfume,
joined by the sweet smell of the first yellow
roses climbing the trellis.
New life is everywhere!

Sweet tastes of honeysuckle,
blooming in abundance throughout the quiet
wood linger until a tart blackberry,
picked off the bush,
causes me to gasp in pleasant surprise.

The dogwood's trunk supports my back,
and the breeze in my hair soothes my spirit.
A tickling sensation on my arm alerts me
to the ant whose home I have
disturbed with a careless sweep of my hand.

Everywhere, the buzz of the bees,
the whispering trees, all sing in sweet accord.
The birds sing along, happy in their wedded bliss.
And my heart sings, too, to be a
part of the earth's spring song.

As day ends, night falls, bringing its own chorus.
The silvery moon sends beams to greet me,
and a star falls that I might make a wish.
"Oh, can every day be like this, free of care?
It's spring and I am glad to be alive!

_____

1. In line 5, "spring assaults the senses," the best synonym for assaults would be:
   A. hits
   B. storms
   C. invades
   D. jumps on

2. In the second stanza, what has "taken flight from my mind?"
   A. dreams
   B. sky
   C. clouds
   D. boughs

3. According to the sixth stanza, which of the following does not "sing in sweet accord"?
   A. bees
   B. birds
   C. trees
   D. wolves

4. What happened to the ant's home?
   A. crushed by the narrator's foot
   B. blown away by a big grasshopper
   C. carried away by a big grasshopper
   D. destroyed by the narrator's hand

Total Problems: Total Correct: Score: © Carson-Dellosa CD-2206

66

Worksheet 67 — Reading a Mileage Chart

Name _____ Reading a Mileage Chart

Refer to the mileage chart to answer each question. Write the answers in the blanks provided.

If you are planning a trip by car, you may want to consult a mileage table like the one below. To read the mileage table: 1) locate one of the cities in the left-hand column; 2) then, go across that row to the column headed by the other city's name. The number shown is the distance in road miles between the two cities.

Road Mileage	Atlanta, GA	Boston, MA	Chicago, IL	Denver, CO	Hartford, CT	Miami, FL	Omaha, NE	Seattle, WA
Albany, NY	991	166	836	1824	108	1405	1284	2909
Boston, MA	1075	X	1015	2003	102	1486	1463	3088
Cleveland, OH	481	648	355	1235	578	1235	803	2428
El Paso, TX	1425	2403	1483	624	2303	1938	1016	1695
Jackson, MS	383	1426	749	1223	1326	908	926	2521
Miami, FL	661	1486	1377	2077	1386	X	1660	3334
Pittsburgh, PA	683	593	472	1460	493	1168	920	2545
Wichita, KS	974	1627	720	515	1527	1608	310	1913

1. How far is it from:

   El Paso to Denver? **624** miles

   Albany to Chicago? **836** miles

   Miami to Atlanta? **661** miles

   Cleveland to Omaha? **803** miles

2. Which city is closest to:

   Jackson? **Atlanta**

   Pittsburgh? **Chicago**

   Albany? **Hartford**

   Wichita? **Omaha**

3. Which city is farthest from:

   Boston? **Seattle**

   Miami? **Seattle**

   El Paso? **Boston**

   Cleveland? **Seattle**

4. Is the distance greater between Albany and Chicago or between Cleveland and Chicago? **Albany and Chicago**

   How much greater? **481** miles

5. How many miles would you travel by road from Boston to Omaha? **1,463** miles

© Carson-Dellosa CD-2206

Total Problems: Total Correct: Score: **67**

Worksheet 68 — Reading a Bar Graph

Name _____ Reading a Bar Graph

Refer to the bar graph to answer each question. Circle the letter beside the correct answer.

Atlanta Middle School — bar graph showing Sports Activity (Softball, Swimming, Basketball, Football, Soccer) vs Number of Students (0–20). Legend: 8th Grade, 7th Grade, 6th Grade.

1. How many more eighth grade students participated in swimming than seventh graders?
   A. 6
   B. 2
   C. 5
   D. 4

2. What was the total number of students that participated in soccer?
   A. 25
   B. 15
   C. 30
   D. 35

3. How many sixth and seventh graders played softball?
   A. 15
   B. 33
   C. 20
   D. 28

4. What was the total number of seventh and eighth graders that played football?
   A. 23
   B. 25
   C. 28
   D. 32

5. How many more sixth grade students participated in basketball than seventh graders?
   A. 6
   B. 10
   C. 8
   D. 12

Total Problems: Total Correct: Score: © Carson-Dellosa CD-2206

68

Name _____   Reading a Line Graph

Refer to the line graph to answer each question. Circle the letter beside the correct answer.

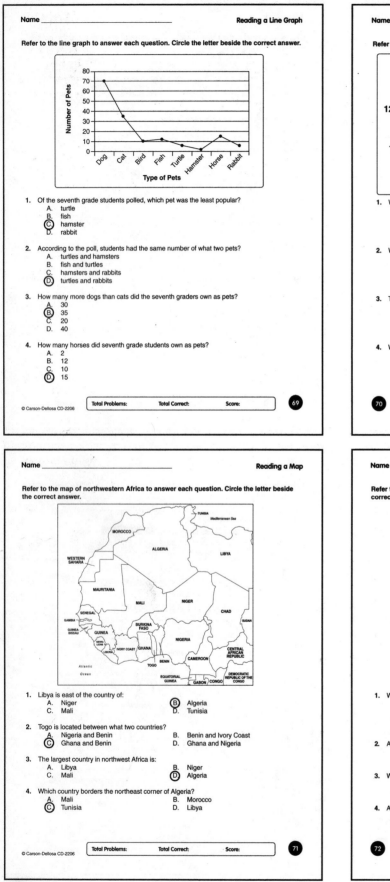

1. Of the seventh grade students polled, which pet was the least popular?
   A. turtle
   B. fish
   C. hamster
   D. rabbit

2. According to the poll, students had the same number of what two pets?
   A. turtles and hamsters
   B. fish and turtles
   C. hamsters and rabbits
   D. turtles and rabbits

3. How many more dogs than cats did the seventh graders own as pets?
   A. 30
   B. 35
   C. 20
   D. 40

4. How many horses did seventh grade students own as pets?
   A. 2
   B. 12
   C. 10
   D. 15

© Carson-Dellosa CD-2206   Total Problems: Total Correct: Score: 69

Name _____   Reading a Pie Graph

Refer to the pie graph to answer each question. Circle the letter beside the correct answer.

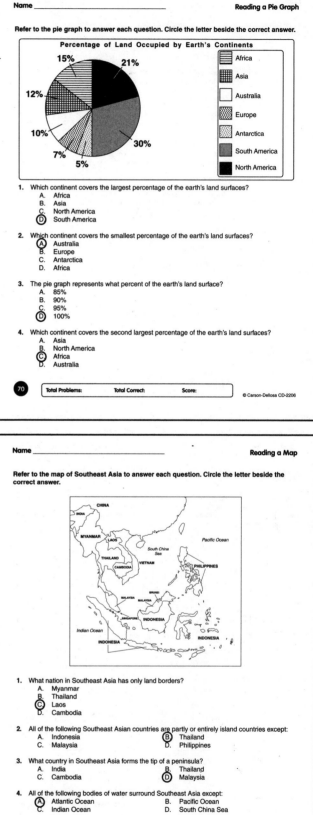

1. Which continent covers the largest percentage of the earth's land surfaces?
   A. Africa
   B. Asia
   C. North America
   D. South America

2. Which continent covers the smallest percentage of the earth's land surfaces?
   A. Australia
   B. Europe
   C. Antarctica
   D. Africa

3. The pie graph represents what percent of the earth's land surface?
   A. 85%
   B. 90%
   C. 95%
   D. 100%

4. Which continent covers the second largest percentage of the earth's land surfaces?
   A. Asia
   B. North America
   C. Africa
   D. Australia

70   Total Problems: Total Correct: Score: © Carson-Dellosa CD-2206

Name _____   Reading a Map

Refer to the map of northwestern Africa to answer each question. Circle the letter beside the correct answer.

1. Libya is east of the country of:
   A. Niger   B. Algeria
   C. Mali   D. Tunisia

2. Togo is located between what two countries?
   A. Nigeria and Benin   B. Benin and Ivory Coast
   C. Ghana and Benin   D. Ghana and Nigeria

3. The largest country in northwest Africa is:
   A. Libya   B. Niger
   C. Mali   D. Algeria

4. Which country borders the northeast corner of Algeria?
   A. Mali   B. Morocco
   C. Tunisia   D. Libya

© Carson-Dellosa CD-2206   Total Problems: Total Correct: Score: 71

Name _____   Reading a Map

Refer to the map of Southeast Asia to answer each question. Circle the letter beside the correct answer.

1. What nation in Southeast Asia has only land borders?
   A. Myanmar
   B. Thailand
   C. Laos
   D. Cambodia

2. All of the following Southeast Asian countries are partly or entirely island countries except:
   A. Indonesia   B. Thailand
   C. Malaysia   D. Philippines

3. What country in Southeast Asia forms the tip of a peninsula?
   A. India   B. Thailand
   C. Cambodia   D. Malaysia

4. All of the following bodies of water surround Southeast Asia except:
   A. Atlantic Ocean   B. Pacific Ocean
   C. Indian Ocean   D. South China Sea

72   Total Problems: Total Correct: Score: © Carson-Dellosa CD-2206

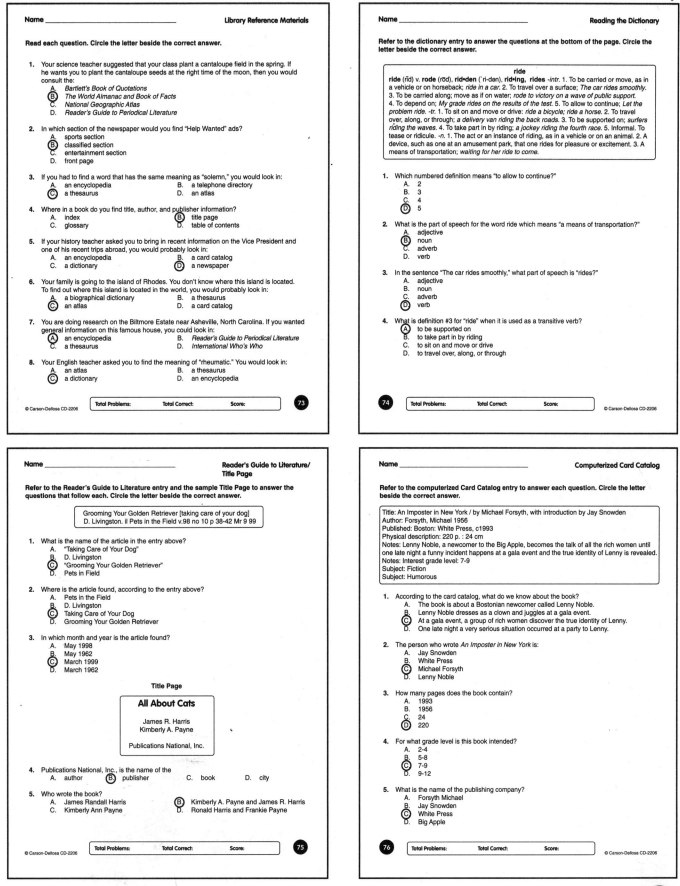

Name _____   Library Reference Materials

Read each question. Circle the letter beside the correct answer.

1. Your science teacher suggested that your class plant a cantaloupe field in the spring. If he wants you to plant the cantaloupe seeds at the right time of the moon, then you would consult:
   A. *Bartlett's Book of Quotations*
   B. *The World Almanac and Book of Facts*
   C. *National Geographic Atlas*
   D. *Reader's Guide to Periodical Literature*

2. In which section of the newspaper would you find "Help Wanted" ads?
   A. sports section
   B. classified section
   C. entertainment section
   D. front page

3. If you had to find a word that has the same meaning as "solemn," you would look in:
   A. an encyclopedia   B. a telephone directory
   C. a thesaurus   D. an atlas

4. Where in a book do you find title, author, and publisher information?
   A. index   B. title page
   C. glossary   D. table of contents

5. If your history teacher asked you to bring in recent information on the Vice President and one of his recent trips abroad, you would probably look in:
   A. an encyclopedia   B. a card catalog
   C. a dictionary   D. a newspaper

6. Your family is going to the island of Rhodes. You don't know where this island is located. To find out where this island is located in the world, you would probably look in:
   A. a biographical dictionary   B. a thesaurus
   C. an atlas   D. a card catalog

7. You are doing research on the Biltmore Estate near Asheville, North Carolina. If you wanted general information on this famous house, you could look in:
   A. an encyclopedia   B. *Reader's Guide to Periodical Literature*
   C. a thesaurus   D. *International Who's Who*

8. Your English teacher asked you to find the meaning of "rheumatic." You would look in:
   A. an atlas   B. a thesaurus
   C. a dictionary   D. an encyclopedia

© Carson-Dellosa CD-2206   Total Problems: Total Correct: Score: **73**

Name _____   Reading the Dictionary

Refer to the dictionary entry to answer the questions at the bottom of the page. Circle the letter beside the correct answer.

> **ride**
> **ride** (rīd) v. **rode** (rōd), **rid•den** (`ri-dən), **rid•ing**, **rides** -*intr.* 1. To be carried or move, as in a vehicle or on horseback; *ride in a car.* 2. To travel over a surface; *The car rides smoothly.* 3. To be carried along; move as if on water; *rode to victory on a wave of public support.* 4. To depend on; *My grade rides on the results of the test.* 5. To allow to continue; *Let the problem ride.* -*tr.* 1. To sit on and move or drive: *ride a bicycle; ride a horse.* 2. To travel over, along, or through; *a delivery van riding the back roads.* 3. To be supported on; *surfers riding the waves.* 4. To take part in by riding; *a jockey riding the fourth race.* 5. Informal. To tease or ridicule. -*n.* 1. The act or an instance of riding, as in a vehicle or on an animal. 2. A device, such as one at an amusement park, that one rides for pleasure or excitement. 3. A means of transportation; *waiting for her ride to come.*

1. Which numbered definition means "to allow to continue?"
   A. 2
   B. 3
   C. 4
   D. 5

2. What is the part of speech for the word *ride* which means "a means of transportation?"
   A. adjective
   B. noun
   C. adverb
   D. verb

3. In the sentence "The car rides smoothly," what part of speech is "rides?"
   A. adjective
   B. noun
   C. adverb
   D. verb

4. What is definition #3 for "ride" when it is used as a transitive verb?
   A. to be supported on
   B. to take part in by riding
   C. to sit on and move or drive
   D. to travel over, along, or through

74   Total Problems: Total Correct: Score: © Carson-Dellosa CD-2206

Name _____   Reader's Guide to Literature/ Title Page

Refer to the Reader's Guide to Literature entry and the sample Title Page to answer the questions that follow each. Circle the letter beside the correct answer.

> Grooming Your Golden Retriever [taking care of your dog]
> D. Livingston. il Pets in the Field v.98 no 10 p 38-42 Mr 9 99

1. What is the name of the article in the entry above?
   A. "Taking Care of Your Dog"
   B. D. Livingston
   C. "Grooming Your Golden Retriever"
   D. Pets in Field

2. Where is the article found, according to the entry above?
   A. Pets in the Field
   B. D. Livingston
   C. Taking Care of Your Dog
   D. Grooming Your Golden Retriever

3. In which month and year is the article found?
   A. May 1998
   B. May 1962
   C. March 1999
   D. March 1962

Title Page

> **All About Cats**
>
> James R. Harris
> Kimberly A. Payne
>
> Publications National, Inc.

4. Publications National, Inc., is the name of the
   A. author   B. publisher   C. book   D. city

5. Who wrote the book?
   A. James Randall Harris   B. Kimberly A. Payne and James R. Harris
   C. Kimberly Ann Payne   D. Ronald Harris and Frankie Payne

© Carson-Dellosa CD-2206   Total Problems: Total Correct: Score: **75**

Name _____   Computerized Card Catalog

Refer to the computerized Card Catalog entry to answer each question. Circle the letter beside the correct answer.

> Title: An Imposter in New York / by Michael Forsyth, with introduction by Jay Snowden
> Author: Forsyth, Michael 1956
> Published: Boston: White Press, c1993
> Physical description: 220 p. : 24 cm
> Notes: Lenny Noble, a newcomer to the Big Apple, becomes the talk of all the rich women until one late night a funny incident happens at a gala event and the true identity of Lenny is revealed.
> Notes: Interest grade level: 7-9
> Subject: Fiction
> Subject: Humorous

1. According to the card catalog, what do we know about the book?
   A. The book is about a Bostonian newcomer called Lenny Noble.
   B. Lenny Noble dresses as a clown and juggles at a gala event.
   C. At a gala event, a group of rich women discover the true identity of Lenny.
   D. One late night a very serious situation occurred at a party to Lenny.

2. The person who wrote *An Imposter in New York* is:
   A. Jay Snowden
   B. White Press
   C. Michael Forsyth
   D. Lenny Noble

3. How many pages does the book contain?
   A. 1993
   B. 1956
   C. 24
   D. 220

4. For what grade level is this book intended?
   A. 2-4
   B. 5-8
   C. 7-9
   D. 9-12

5. What is the name of the publishing company?
   A. Forsyth Michael
   B. Jay Snowden
   C. White Press
   D. Big Apple

76   Total Problems: Total Correct: Score: © Carson-Dellosa CD-2206

Left Worksheet

Name _____   Reading a Table of Contents

Refer to the table of contents below to answer the questions. Circle the letter beside the correct answer.

1. If your teacher asked you to create a travel brochure on the Blowing Rock, NC, you could probably find information on creating the travel brochure on what page?
   A. 16   (B) 44   C. 64   D. 57

2. If you were seeking information on the origination of blue grass music, in which chapter would you most likely find the information?
   A. The Appalachian Mountains
   B. Chimney Rock, NC
   (C) Appalachian Culture
   D. Appalachian People

3. From which entry would the following passage most likely come? "Most of the Appalachians have rocky soil. In valleys, where the soil richer and more fertile, farmers grow tobacco."
   A. Tourist Attractions
   B. Local Events
   C. Where to Stay
   (D) Geography of the Appalachians

Total Problems: ___   Total Correct: ___   Score: ___   **77**

Right Worksheet

Name _____   Reading an Index

Refer to the index to answer the questions at the bottom of the page. Circle the letter beside each correct answer.

INDEX

C
Cambodia 33, 44
Campaign for Nuclear Disarmament 50
Canada 5, 23
capitalism 15, 29, 56
Castro, Fidel 37, 39
Central America 36-37
Chernobyl 47, 53
Chiang Kai-shek 16
children's rights 51
Chile 36
China 16-17, 25, 39, 40-41, 47-50
Cultural Revolution 41, revolution 16
Churchill, Winston 27-29
Civil Rights Movement 50-51, 56
Clinton, William 43
Cold War 38-39, 52, 54, 56

Columbia 36
communication 5
Communism, See Soviet Union
computers 53
concentration camps 25, 27, 29
Cuba 37, 39, 47
Cultural Revolution 41
Czechoslovakia 22, 28, 39, 47
Czech Republic 47

D
Dalai Lama 40
D-Day 26
de Gaulle, Charles 26
democracy 19, 41, 44, 40-51, 55-56

1. If you wanted to find information on China's Cultural Revolution, on what page(s) would you look?
   A. 16-17   B. 47-50   (C) 41   D. 25

2. If you were interested in learning more about capitalism, on what page(s) would you look?
   (A) 15, 29, 56   B. 5, 23   C. 36-37   D. 47, 53

3. What page(s) would probably give you information about Winston Churchill?
   A. 40-41   B. 16   C. 50   (D) 27-29

4. If you were writing a research paper on concentration camps, on what page(s) would you look?
   A. 23, 25, 27   (B) 25, 27, 29   C. 37, 39, 47   D. 22, 28, 39

5. Which one of the following statements about the index is not true?
   A. Information on China can be found in at least 10 places.
   B. Each topic is followed by a page number where the information can be found.
   (C) The index gives definitions of words and phrases.
   D. The topics are listed alphabetically.

78   Total Problems: ___   Total Correct: ___   Score: ___